HOW TO
RETIRE
IN A
WEEKEND

A 3-day guide to navigating the path from "Burnt Out" to "I'm Out!"

Andie Doller
& Curvin Miller IV

With Foreword by Rob Russell

Copyright © 2024 by Curvin Miller IV and Andie Doller.

All rights reserved. No part of this publication may be reproduced, distributed, or transmitted in any form or by any means, including photocopying, recording, or other electronic or mechanical methods, without the prior written permission of the publisher, except in the case of brief quotations embodied in critical reviews and certain other noncommercial uses permitted by copyright law. For permission requests, write to the publisher at the address below. These materials are provided to you by Curvin Miller IV and Andie Doller for informational purposes only, and Curvin Miller IV and Andie Doller expressly disclaim any and all liability arising out of or relating to your use of same. The provision of these materials does not constitute legal or investment advice and does not establish an attorney-client relationship between you and Curvin Miller IV and Andie Doller. No tax advice is contained in these materials. You are solely responsible for ensuring the accuracy and completeness of all materials as well as the compliance, validity, and enforceability of all materials under any applicable law. The advice and strategies found within may not be suitable for every situation. You are expressly advised to consult with a qualified attorney or other professional in making any such determination and to determine your legal or financial needs. No warranty of any kind, implied, expressed, or statutory, including but not limited to the warranties of title and non-infringement of third-party rights, is given with respect to this publication.

Curvin Miller IV and Andie Doller/Russell Total Wealth and Wellness
One Russell Place, Dayton, OH 45409
www.totalwealthadvice.com

How to Retire in a Weekend/Curvin Miller IV and Andie Doller — 2nd edition

ISBN 9798371499721

Curvin Miller IV and Andie Doller are registered as Investment Advisor Representatives and are licensed insurance agents in the state of Ohio. Russell Total Wealth and Wellness is an independent financial services firm that helps individuals create retirement strategies using a variety of investment and insurance products to custom suit their needs and objectives.

Insurance products are offered through the insurance business Russell Total Wealth and Wellness. Russell Total Wealth and Wellness is also an Investment Advisory practice that offers products and services through AE Wealth Management, LLC (AEWM), a Registered Investment Adviser. AEWM does not offer insurance products. The insurance products offered by Russell Total Wealth and Wellness are not subject to Investment Adviser requirements. The contents of this book are provided for informational purposes only and are not intended to serve as the basis for any financial decisions. Any tax, legal, or estate planning information is general in nature. Please remember that converting an employer plan account to a Roth IRA is a taxable event. Increased taxable income from the Roth IRA conversion may have several consequences. Be sure to consult with a qualified tax advisor before making any decisions regarding your IRA. It should not be construed as legal or tax advice. Always consult an attorney or tax professional regarding the applicability of this information to your unique situation.

Information presented is believed to be factual and up-to-date, but we do not guarantee its accuracy, and it should not be regarded as a complete analysis of the subjects discussed. All expressions of opinion are those of the author as of the date of publication and are subject to change. Content should not be construed as personalized investment advice nor should it be interpreted as an offer to buy or sell any securities mentioned. A financial advisor should be consulted before implementing any of the strategies presented.

Investing involves risk, including the potential loss of principal. No investment strategy can guarantee a profit or protect against loss in periods of declining values. Any references to protection benefits or guaranteed/lifetime income streams refer only to fixed insurance products, not securities or investment products. Annuity guarantees rely on financial strength and claims-paying ability of issuing insurance company. Annuities are insurance products that may be subject to fees, surrender charges, and holding periods, which vary by carrier. Annuities are not FDIC insured. Russell Total Wealth and Wellness is not affiliated with the U.S. government or any governmental agency. Any media logos and/or trademarks contained herein are the property of their respective owners and no endorsement by those owners of Russell Total Wealth and Wellness is stated or implied. Total Wealth and Wellness is a paid radio show.

This How-To Guide is not intended to be a one size fits all solution; as every retirement situation is specific to the individual or couple. Investments involve risk including the potential loss of principal invested. References to protection, safety, lifetime income, generally refer to fixed insurance products. Insurance guarantees are backed by the financial strength and claims paying abilities of the issuing carrier. Any names used in the examples presented in this book is using a fictional couple as a hypothetical example for illustrative purposes only; it does not represent a real life scenario, and should not be construed as advice designed to meet the particular needs of an individual's situation.

Table of Contents

How to Retire in a Weekend i
Friday Evening: Do I Really Want to Do This? 1
Saturday Morning: Can I Afford This? 7
Saturday Afternoon: Income Planning 15
Saturday Evening: What's the Risk? 25
Saturday Night (Late): A Taxing Issue 39
Sunday Morning: Estate & Legacy Planning 53
Sunday Afternoon: Affording Health Care & Long-Term Care 65
Sunday Night: The Road Ahead 81
Frequently Asked Questions, and Some Answers 87
Choosing Your Guide on the Road Through Retirement 105
Acknowledgments 113
About the Authors 117

FOREWORD

How to Retire in a Weekend

By Rob Russell
**FOUNDER/CEO, and Investment Advisor Representative
RUSSELL TOTAL WEALTH AND WELLNESS**

I sometimes get strange looks from people when I first mention my contention that our current concept of retirement is a relatively new thing.

"Are you serious?" they might ask. "People have been stepping away from work since the first caveman finally got fed up with pounding stone into wheels."

Well, they did and they didn't. For centuries, people worked until they could work no longer. Many worked until they dropped, sometimes right there on the factory floor or all alone on the north forty. Our idea of "planning for retirement," quite frankly, has only been around for decades as opposed to centuries.

Think about it. Social Security was implemented as recently as 1936 as part of President Franklin Roosevelt's efforts to recover from the Great Depression. It was designed, in part, to provide a safety net that might induce older workers to retire and open their hard-to-find jobs to younger workers. That simply wasn't done in the days of bread lines and dust bowls. If you had a job then, you held onto it until they pried you away.

In the years that followed, retirement was a simpler process. The government provided Social Security and many companies offered pensions, often as a way of inducing employee loyalty. Retirement income was often depicted as a steady, three-legged stool of Social

Security, company-provided pension payments, and any retirement savings a worker had put away on their own.

But that picture began to change in the early 1980s.

The "defined benefit plan" – aka, a pension – began to die out beginning in 1978 with a little-noticed change in the IRS tax code, section 401(k), which allowed employees to avoid being taxed on "deferred compensation." This change didn't get a lot of immediate attention. It wasn't until two years later that a benefits consultant developed the idea of the "defined contribution plan" as an alternative to the traditional pension. Employees would contribute to their own retirement plan, get an immediate tax break for doing so, and usually receive some employer match (at whatever level the company chose to contribute) in return. Today, most people consider this to be a good deal, but it took several years before the idea of workers funding their own retirement through tax-deferred plans such as the 401(k) was embraced by both employees and employers who, frankly, were tired of funding pension programs.

But along with the idea of workers funding their own retirement came some complexities.

Now that we were basically on our own when it came to funding a significant part of our retirement, we were expected to become experts on the subject. In addition to being skilled at our job and being a great spouse or parent, we now also had to become well versed on matters involving our retirement. How much can I afford to set aside from each paycheck? How should I invest that money? How will I go about taking money from these savings when it comes time to do so? And, by the way, won't I have to pay tax on all this cash eventually?

Such questions created a demand and need for retirement planning help, a need so great that an entire huge industry has been built up to meet it. The key word here is retirement "planning" which is considerably more involved than just retirement "saving." I'd guess that if one were to check the number of books related to retirement planning that are available today on Amazon, there would be tens of thousands of titles.

This book, needless to note, is yet another. But one with, I believe, a very unique approach.

It needn't be that difficult

My name is Rob Russell, founder, CEO and Investment Advisor Representative of Russell Total Wealth and Wellness, my Dayton, Ohio-based company with clients throughout the country. I've asked two of my most trusted associates, Ohio natives Curvin Miller and Andie Doller, to create this book to help simplify the process of making one's retirement decision – something our company has been doing with people for over 20 years.

Hence, our title, *How to Retire in a Weekend*.

Our premise here will be simple. That is, it's hard to become an expert on retirement, and you shouldn't beat yourself up if you aren't. Not when there are people available – people such as Curvin and Andie and my entire team – who can help guide you along this new path on your life's journey. And not when there are easier steps to take – steps that can be completed over a 3-day weekend – that can help you to determine whether now (or some point in the near future) is the time to take the plunge into what should be one of the most exciting and fulfilling phases of your life.

What will make this book different from the thousands of other retirement self-help books written by thousands of retirement planners? I believe there are two things:

First, I believe too many other authors and retirement gurus make the decision-making process more difficult than it has to be. In the following chapters, Curvin and Andie will examine the simple steps we take with our clients to help provide them the confidence to know that they're ready to make their retirement decision at a time of their choosing. We'll look at several key issues and questions that can be addressed – if not resolved – over the concentrated course of a weekend.

The other thing that's different about this book is our effort to help people figure out the most important part of their retirement plan, something not all planners focus on: what you are going to do with your retirement. What will a perfect day in retirement look like for you? What are your goals, your dreams, your essential needs, or your discretionary wants? Determining these expectations, is a necessary first component in developing the financial side of your retirement plan, something we will help develop once you decide exactly where you want to go.

OK, I hear you.

You're likely thinking at this point that nothing as involved as retirement planning can be simple. You're thinking that you've worked hard for thirty, forty years or more to (perhaps) raise a family, grow wealth, or save/invest for your future by putting away whatever you could whenever you could afford to do so. And now you've got "retirement money" stashed away in various places – an IRA here, a 401(k) there, maybe a 403(b) or a TSP or SEP account somewhere else. You may have an annuity or two, and probably some life insurance you haven't looked at in years. Your financial affairs more closely resemble a kitchen or garage utility drawer: you know a lot of helpful tools are in there somewhere, even if you don't know how all of them work.

Well, the only way I know to find exactly what you have in life is to start looking. So, let's begin.

People often make this process more complex than it needs to be. Really, you can easily go through a checklist of things you can find out for yourself. You can, for example, go to www.SocialSecurity.gov and learn what your monthly benefit will be, depending on when you start taking it. You can easily review the retirement savings and investment accounts you have – where they are, how much is there, what is their tax status between qualified (tax-deferred) or non-qualified (taxable now). Are these assets in stocks, bonds, mutual funds, or annuities?

This is all part of defining the foundation, walls, and roof of what we call our "Fiscal House," a concept we'll discuss throughout this book. These will be the crucial first steps in truly understanding how much you've saved because, frankly, many people have no idea.

As mentioned earlier, our company has spent over twenty years helping people put together the pieces of their financial puzzle. Your different retirement savings plans – your annuities, your bank accounts, your Social Security – are all like pieces of the puzzle. To piece them together, you typically need the puzzle box cover that shows you what the finished picture is supposed to look like.

Yet many people try to put things together without that kind of help, and that's a challenge. There's just too much craziness going on in the world with rising taxes, inflation, and stock market volatility – evergreen issues that will never go away – to try to put all those pieces together on your own.

This is where a team of retirement planners such as mine comes into play. But first, you must see the picture – the puzzle box cover –of what your retirement can look like. And thus begins the long weekend.

The three-day plan

Throughout the course of this book, Curvin and Andie will break down in greater detail the elements that should be evaluated in a three-day process that looks ahead to your immediate future. But first, let's do a brief preview of what our "weekend" might look like.

"Friday" is our day for taking personal inventory of where you stand today. What is your motivation for wanting to retire? Has your work, health, or life situation gotten to the point that you want to step away from the workforce this Monday, or a month from now? Six months maybe, or even six years? Do you merely **want** to walk away, or do you feel you **need** to do so?

Maybe you just want to know whether you are in position to step away now or at any other time of your choosing. To know this, you'll first have to answer the all-important question, "Can I afford to retire right now?"

We'll address this issue Saturday when we have an entire day – a heavy-lifting day – to take a deep-dive look at what you can expect in retirement income.

This is the day we begin to develop a blueprint for your Fiscal House. This is the day to gather up all recent financial statements – some of which you probably haven't examined in years – to determine what you've actually saved for retirement. Some people are pleasantly surprised to see the result. Others, not so much.

This also is the day to explore what you can expect to receive each month in "fixed income," the regular, reliable income from Social Security, annuity, dividend, and interest payments that forms the "foundation" of your Fiscal House.

This also is the day to consider what your monthly budget might look like in retirement. What will you spend on regular living expenses? What will you spend on the "frill" things you've dreamed of doing in retirement? How will you pay for these expenses from your fixed-income foundation, and what kind of drawdown from your retirement savings might be required to fill any income gaps?

There will be other budget items to consider. How will you manage rising health care costs in retirement? What might you pay in health insurance premiums, either before or after becoming eligible for Medicare? What are the tax implications of the money you've saved? How much of your 401(k) is yours to keep, and how much will go to Uncle Sam? Have you considered inflation – a huge factor, even in 2024 as consumers continue to recover from a 2022 surge that reached 9.1 percent in June 2022[1]– in adjusting your budget on an annual basis?

Yeah, it's a long day.

Sunday is the "finishing day." Your Fiscal House blueprint is established. You have a foundation of stable, sustainable income. You have supporting walls of additional income from your retirement savings. But you still have to work on the roof, your means of producing future income or sheltering your loved ones. This might involve beginning to think about an estate plan that provides for people you care about when you are no longer here to do so.

It's also the time to think about where you go from here.

The goal by the end of our weekend is to have a more complete picture of your retirement future than you had on Friday afternoon. What you do with this view will likely depend on what you've seen.

I've known people, especially those who've done a good job of saving for their future and investing in themselves, who after a weekend of taking personal inventory may have a better understanding of where they are at in their retirement journey.

Others will see that they have more work to do, that their retirement outlook is just too grey right now. They're in a middle zone and need more answers to their questions. They need help.

But at least they've come to that understanding. They know more on Sunday night than they knew on Friday afternoon, and that's a start. They know more about where they need to go, and they have a better understanding of what to do to get there. They have a blueprint at the very least. They may not be ready to start building just yet, but as Curvin

---

[1] Lucia Mutikani. Reuters. May 15, 2024. "US consumer inflation resumes downward trend as domestic demand cools" https://www.reuters.com/markets/us/us-consumer-prices-rise-less-than-expected-april-core-cpi-slows-2024-05-15/

and Andie will point out, there can still be time to help such people fulfill their retirement plans once they have a realistic look at what they stand.

Clearly, some of the ideas we'll discuss in the following chapters will take more than a three-day weekend to implement. Developing a retirement tax-efficient strategy, for instance, sometimes involves working with a CPA to get a complete understanding of where you are in your current tax bracket and how future retirement taxes might affect that.

Truthfully, the timeline doesn't matter as much as simply beginning the process. Whether it takes you three days or three months to become comfortable with your retirement decision, the point of this book is to help you compress the elements of that decision-making process into as small a time period as possible. With this in mind, I invite you to come spend the weekend with us and our book.

CHAPTER 1

Friday Evening: Do I Really Want to Do This?

Imagine it's a Friday evening, getting close to 5 o'clock, and Jeannie is tempted to pour something "tall and strong." However, she resists the temptation.

The school week has worn down the sixty-two-year-old teacher, a thirty-year veteran educator – she stepped away for a decade when her own children were young. Her third-grade class is, for the most part, a good group of kids, but eight-year-olds will always be, you know, eight-year-olds.

Teaching is a bit better than a few years ago when the still-emerging Covid crisis put her school into near total lockdown. Teaching virtually for almost a year was one of the most difficult things Jeannie had ever done. Taking preventative measures to ward off her own exposure to the virus didn't make things easier. Watching a dear friend nearly lose a battle with the virus – it was touch-and-go for a long while – affected her deeply. And now, the kids seem somehow different upon their return to full-time in-class instruction.

Jeannie loves her students, always will. Yet, now she wonders if it might be time to walk away from this work.

Her husband Tom, two years older, is thinking the same thing at the same time.

Unlike Jeannie, who is treasured by her co-workers and could work forever at her school should she so choose, Tom is beginning to feel the sting of agism in his workplace. He has less and less in common with younger co-workers who seem to be getting the lucrative assignments that were once his domain. He's watched in recent years as older workers, people of roughly the age he is now, were "encouraged" to take early-retirement buyouts. Tom wonders if it won't soon be his turn to be called into the HR office, a suspicion that grows with every word his boss ***doesn't*** say to him.

Tom fixes the first of the two cocktails he allows himself on an occasional Friday evening. Such "occasions" seem to be coming more frequently these days.

"I think I'm finally ready to walk away from it," he says to Jeannie, reviving a conversation they've had several times in the past few years. "This time, I really think I'm ready to talk to the boss come Monday."

"I hear you," she replies. "But do this for me, will you? Take the weekend and think about it. For that matter, let's both think about it. You may not be the only one giving notice next week."

Begin the voyage of self-discovery

Jeannie and Tom are, as you likely guessed, fictional names for people facing very real-life decisions. We will continue to reference them, but remember, they represent a fictitious couple. For years they've talked about, as well as saved and invested for, a time when they could walk away from the daily rat race and enter a world in which their time would be completely their own. Yet now that this time is staring them in the face, they have understandable doubts about whether they are truly ready to take the first big steps into the potentially exciting yet unfamiliar world of retirement.

We – Sr. Vice President and Sr. Wealth Advisor Curvin Miller and Sr. Wealth Advisor Andie Doller – see people like Jeannie and Tom every day in our Russell Total Wealth and Wellness offices in Dayton, Ohio.

Many of our first-visit clients have heard us talk on WHIO Radio in Dayton, or on other local and national TV broadcasts, or in a Total Wealth Live event about our belief that making one's retirement decision can be simplified to the point of potentially resolving the issue over a three-day weekend. Our company president, CEO and Investment Advisor Representative, Rob Russell describes this belief with his saying, "It's entirely possible to go from burnout to 'I'm out' in three days."

Some people are skeptical, no doubt, upon hearing this. There's no way, they say, that something as complicated as making a decision about the rest of your life can be done that quickly.

Well, Jeannie and Tom are about to test our theory. And we'll be here to guide them along the way.

Before we start this journey, however, there are some things you should know about our boss and how his philosophy has helped shape our own approaches.

We believe that Rob Russell approaches retirement planning from a different perspective than most other financial advisors throughout America. We've heard him talk many times about how too many advisors put too much emphasis on what he calls, "counting the commas and zeros on your account statements." The traditional approach of growing retirement savings to some "magic number," and then deciding what to do with that money, is backwards in Rob's opinion, an opinion we happen to share.

"It's like getting in your car with no idea of where you're going, then wondering whether you'll have enough gas to get there," he says. "I think it's more important to first ask, 'Get where? Where are you going?' We must know where you want to go and why you want to go there *before* we can talk about what route to take along the way."

Putting Rob's "road trip" analogy in plain terms, we believe it's more important to start any retirement planning with the vision of what you want your retirement to look like. Once you've developed a reasonable expectation of what that might be, we can begin to do the financial planning necessary to help make it happen.

Retirement visions, after all, affect retirement income needs. Please don't misunderstand us. You've earned the right to enjoy yourself in retirement, and we want you to do that. But how much and what types of "enjoyment" might you afford? Do you have dreams of traveling to the beautiful rolling hills around Dublin, Ireland or staying closer to home for the famous Jack Nicklaus golf courses around Dublin, Ohio? Do you have dreams of owning a second "snowbird" home in Florida or Arizona or just taking extended winter vacations in a warmer climate?

It's with these "big picture" thoughts in mind that we begin our "weekend" with Jeannie and Tom.

Taking your personal inventory: What matters most to you?

The couple's first concern, they will tell you immediately, is whether they can afford the retirement of their dreams. Please believe us when we say we're going to spend a considerable bit of time talking about this very thing in our next two chapters, the "Saturday morning and afternoon" portion of our weekend. But before we do that, here are some questions we would have you consider before going through this journey:

Are you truly ready to take the plunge into retirement? Is this something you really want or need to do? And if so, why?

We ask this with the belief that everyone should have a good motivation for wanting to make one of the biggest decisions in life. This is, after all, a transition some people are not comfortable making. Here's why we say that:

Many people we visit with have worked hard daily for thirty-five to forty or more years. What will such work-oriented people, God love 'em, do with themselves and all their new-found "free time?" What will they do when the alarm doesn't ring from Monday through Friday, when suddenly every day of the week is a Saturday? What will a great day in retirement look like to people more used to keeping their nose to the grindstone? How do you suddenly go on cruise control when you've spent a lifetime with your foot on the gas?

"Ah, don't worry about us," Tom and Jeannie might well respond. "We'll find plenty to keep us busy: watching the grandkids, spending time with old friends and hobbies, traveling, or even taking a nap whenever we want to."

By this point, the couple seems highly motivated to embrace retirement.

Different people find their motivation in different ways and places. Maybe, like Jeannie, you're burned out after years of fighting the same battles – troubled kids, even more troubling parents, administrators who've forgotten what it means to be in the classroom. Maybe the stress, the frustration, the daily aggravation becomes too much. Maybe you're ready to try something completely different, perhaps on a part-time or volunteer basis. Maybe you just need an extended break, one that might last twenty, twenty-five, thirty or more years.

Or maybe, like Tom, you feel yourself being nudged toward the door. Maybe health concerns – either your own or that of, say, an elderly parent who needs continual help – factors in your decision. Maybe you want or need to reduce stress or be in more control over your own time. Maybe you want to get your life back on your schedule instead of someone else's.

And maybe your priorities have changed in recent years.

We've heard lately from many different clients that Covid changed their outlooks on life, especially when it comes to spending time with family or enriching their lives through something other than a paycheck. The world has changed from what we knew at the start of 2020, and maybe your personal outlook on life has changed as well, particularly if you, a loved one, or anyone else close to you had to deal with Covid. That can be a trigger that causes some to say, "I'm going to walk away from a routine, even if it means walking away from a regular paycheck and all that I've known for the past forty years. Even if it means taking a step into the unknown."

But that kind of resolve requires motivation. And that's why the first questions you need to ask yourself as you take time to consider your future on a Friday night include, "Why do I want to do this? What are my goals? What do I want to accomplish?"

If you are comfortable with your reasons and motives for wanting to retire after completing this personal inventory, please continue with us in the following chapters. We'll have plenty of other points to ponder and questions to ask yourself during this weekend. Among them:

How will I provide a paycheck now that I'm no longer receiving one? How will I pay for health care insurance until Medicare kicks in? How will I pay for what Medicare doesn't cover, including the possibility of long-term nursing care? How can I continue growing what I've saved without exposing it all to market risk? How will I support a spouse or have something to give to my kids when I'm no longer here?

Yeah, we'll get to all that in the next two days.

If, however, you are still not sure you're mentally ready to take the retirement leap, please press ahead with us anyway. The things we will cover over the weekend will help you someday, and likely someday soon. Even if you're not ready to make "the call" on Monday, the information in the following chapters will help you with your retirement decision whether it comes in the next three weeks, three months, or three years.

For now, relax a bit and take some time with your thoughts. We've got a busy day scheduled for Saturday, one that will involve a good bit of important research for your future. The process may seem daunting, but it doesn't have to be. We promise, there will be time to watch the Ohio State Buckeyes in the afternoon or the Columbus Blue Jackets later in the evening.

It's been said, and we believe with a great deal of accuracy, that people spend more time planning vacations than they do their retirement. Well, come Saturday we're going to plan a vacation. The longest vacation you will ever take.

Get a good night's sleep. We'll see you in the morning. Feel free to sleep in.

CHAPTER 2

Saturday Morning: Can I Afford This?

Good Saturday morning to you. Hope you slept well. Had breakfast yet? A chance to review the morning news either online or – and we hope this doesn't date us – by reading the morning paper? Did you walk the dog yet? Feed the cat? Did you have your morning coffee or orange juice? Maybe even a second cup?

Good. Now, brew a fresh pot. We've got a big day ahead of us, one that might just open your eyes to what the rest of your life might look like.

After having spent Friday evening taking inventory of your personal feelings and motivations, we'll now spend much of today taking inventory of your financial situation. To put that another way, now that we've addressed the question, "Do I really want to retire, either real soon or someday soon?" we'll now move on to several equally important questions. Foremost among them: "Can I afford to retire at this point?"

To answer this question, we first need a bare-bones accounting of what you've actually put away for retirement, either as an individual or a couple. Simply put, do the numbers add up in support of my desire to retire soon? Have I done the right preparation, or is there more work yet to be done? Where do I stand now financially? What does my current situation say about my future?

We would suggest from experience that most people, maybe even you, have no real idea of what their "retirement nest egg" truly looks like. We're about to help them find out.

This process will begin with gathering up the most recent statements you can find for your retirement savings, investment, and bank accounts. If you own or have an interest in a business, what might it be worth? If you own property, a recent estimate of its worth is helpful. And while you're digging, look for recent statements showing the cash value and death benefits available on any life insurance policies that remain active. This information will come in handy as the weekend progresses.

Now, if you are like a lot of people we know, all this information is likely scattered here and there. Like many, you probably haven't looked at some of these documents in a long time. There may even be some accounts you forgot you had, unlikely as that seems. It's not uncommon, for example, for people who had a 401(k) with a former employer early in their working career to overlook this potential source of retirement income. Really, we see it happen! Out of sight, out of mind is more than a cliché.

(This presents a reason for "rolling over" a 401(k) into either a personal IRA or a new defined-contribution plan when switching jobs. But that's a story for another time and a later chapter.)

Finding all these documents will be easier for some people than others. Those who've organized their financial lives into spreadsheets or separate folders in a file cabinet will likely find the material they need quickly. Our congratulations if we've just described your organizational abilities.

Others will have to do some digging for long-overlooked paperwork or account information stored online. Don't be surprised if you have to use the "forgot your password" function more than once for your online accounts. Don't get discouraged. Keep plugging away. You'll eventually be glad you did.

Sure, some of this will seem like a scavenger hunt. But try to stay positive. Think of this instead as a hunt for lost treasure because that's exactly what it is. You are quite literally working to put together the scattered puzzle pieces of your financial life.

Here's another way to look at it. You, or someone you love, is going to have to do this work eventually. Come age seventy-three (or age seventy-five if you were born in 1960 or later), the IRS will compel you to begin taking Required Minimum Distributions from tax-deferred retirement accounts you've been growing for years. You'll need to know where these accounts are and how much is in them to avoid a costly penalty. You also don't want your grieving survivors having to search for this stuff when they inherit the untaxed balance of your IRAs or have to go looking for insurance policies or financial statements. We'll address these concerns more in depth in a later chapter.

Look, we're not doing a major accounting project here. We're not preparing a report to the IRS. You don't have to "show your work," and there is no penalty for under- or over-reporting your net worth.

Still, this is a housekeeping project you should complete – if not now, then soon. So, why not now on this weekend you've designated for taking a detailed financial look at your future, at your retirement.

More than a mental accounting

Why is all this important?

Well, we're going to look in the next chapter – shortly after lunch in our "weekend" planning session – at the all-important issue of income planning in retirement. What might you expect in recurring monthly expenses? How will you create an emergency fund? What kind of "fun" things do you hope to do? How will you pay for all this once your regular paycheck stops? What might you expect from "fixed income," and how will you cover any gap between recurring expenses and regular income with money from your retirement savings?

We're getting ahead of ourselves. For now, let's concentrate on looking at what you've done with your financial life to this point, then begin thinking about what this might mean for the major life transition that is to follow.

This is the time to take more than what we've come to call a "mental accounting" of our financial status. Often, we merely add the numbers up in our head, especially when it comes to taking an account of our assets. This can be potentially risky. We make a lot of assumptions, and some of them can be wrong when we may not have all our facts straight.

That's why it's important to have a more accurate accounting of what you've saved for retirement and any other income-producing assets you have. Now is when all those monthly account statements become more than just reports you likely seldom (if ever) read. Now is when you look hard at those numbers and ask, "Will I have the means to retire, not just in the first years, but over this full period of twenty, twenty-five, thirty, or more years?"

This involves more than just amassing wealth and meeting some arbitrary "magic retirement number." The emphasis soon will be on finding ways to take income from those assets. The figures on those monthly statements now represent money – actual cash – you will need to last as long as you do. These once-abstract figures, all those commas and zeroes, are about to become a part of your income that will provide the means to live whatever lifestyle you can afford.

But the first step in doing this is to replace your mental accounting with hard, cold facts. You need to start looking at some actual numbers and do some real, tangible accounting. People may have an idea in their heads of where they stand financially, but they can't remember the last time they took a real look at their 401(k) statement or checked the death benefit and designated beneficiaries on a life insurance policy. It's not until they start digging up their financial statements or looking up passwords to log into their accounts online that they get a more accurate picture of where they stand.

Again, this research can seem a little overwhelming. It's the part in the planning process where a lot of people shut down. Maybe they don't know how to go finding their financial statements or just haven't taken time to organize these things. Like it or not, you'll have to do this financial-archeology eventually – that upcoming RMD thing, remember? – and it doesn't have to be as daunting as it may seem. It just takes some time, and you've set aside this weekend.

The "a-ha" moment at the bottom line

Getting a more complete look at your pre-retirement Fiscal House could involve more than just your savings and investments. Other physical "credits" on your account ledger might also be considered, as well as any debits.

A realistic estimate of the value of your home, or of your equity in it if you still have a mortgage, should figure somewhere in the total value of your assets. This is especially true if you might be wanting to move.

Maybe you plan to downsize. Maybe you want to move into a retirement village. Maybe you'd like to live in a different – dare we say, warmer? – part of the country. The current value of your home could have an impact on any future housing decision, so it's good to get an idea of the estimate as part of your financial inventory.

You should also consider the debt side of the equation.

Now, debt should not be the overriding factor in your retirement decision. That said, it's important to note that some debt issues can potentially sink a retirement plan in a heartbeat.

This doesn't mean that you can't take debt into retirement, but you do have to manage it. Keep in mind that we're talking about "normal" debt here. Taking a mortgage into retirement is normal debt. Making car payments in retirement is normal. But having a lot of high-interest credit card debt? Still paying off student loans for your children? That's not normal.

You should separate good debt from bad debt, and some people have trouble doing that. We sometimes hear people say, "I can't even think about retirement just yet because I've got a lot of debt. I can't retire until the day I'm debt-free."

But, realistically, that day may never come. Or, it may not make financial sense if you give up too much in an effort to be debt-free. This might be the case if you were to take for example, say, $200,000 out of the $500,000 in your 401(k) just to pay off your mortgage. And yet we see this done occasionally by well-intentioned people who told themselves they must have their mortgage paid off before they retire.

It's a noble goal, but not necessarily an essential one. Another example, you may have let's say seven years remaining on a mortgage with a $100,000 balance and carrying a 2 percent interest rate, a not uncommon rate before the interest rate hikes of 2022. We would be OK with that kind of debt, providing of course that a client can afford the monthly payments.

And now, after a productive morning, we come to the bottom line. You've added up all the numbers from your research, and now you can see in black-and-white the net result of what you (or you and a spouse) have spent your life working, saving, and investing to produce.

This is a moment of reckoning for many people, what we call the "a-ha moment." Many people we meet are pleasantly surprised at what they see; they did better than they imagined in preparing for retirement. You can almost sense a lightbulb being switched on as they realize, often for the first time, "Hey, we can really retire whenever we want." We're happy for them, truly.

But other people, sadly, don't get to experience the "a-ha moment." Some don't make the effort to gather up their statements or make a call or log-in to an online account to find where they stand. Some are disappointed by what they see when they do add things up.

If this is you, we encourage you to not be overly dismayed. A less-than-promising picture today doesn't mean it has to stay that way forever. Our Retirement Planners at Russell Total Wealth and Wellness will work with clients to help improve their retirement outlook if needed.

There is always time, we believe, to make adjustments. Maybe those adjustments mean working longer, or delaying Social Security to enhance the benefit, or potentially maximize contributions to your IRA or 401(k). There are always steps that can be taken to help you along the road to retirement, even when stumbling at the start.

But those steps can't be taken without an honest evaluation of where you stand today, the starting point in your journey. And the only way to determine that – to borrow from the famous Nike slogan – is to "just do it."

For Tom and Jeannie, the "a-ha" moment comes when they calculate their total retirement "nest egg" at $1.7 million – far, far more than they ever thought possible when they first began putting away a few dollars from every paycheck as an investment in their future. That figure does not include the estimated value of their home or the $50,000 bank balance they routinely maintain as their "emergency cash" resource.

Tom, a career-long defense contractor who works closely with projects at nearby Wright-Patterson Air Force Base, has managed to invest and grow some $1.25 million in his company's 401(k). Jeannie, knowing that as an Ohio teacher, she would receive a state-funded pension in lieu of Social Security benefits, invested and grew another $200,000 in a 403(b)-retirement account available to public employees.

The couple also made a decision Saturday morning regarding an inherited residence they've been using for rental income.

Tom once thought he'd spend his retirement managing several different income-producing rental properties. But in recent years, he's changed his mind. Rental collections and making repairs were often a challenge in the best of times, and during the Covid pandemic made collections even more difficult. Tom has had it with what some landlords call the "evil Ts" – taxes, tenants, and toilets.

He and Jeannie have decided to sell the rental property. They believe they can get $250,000 for the house (it needs work), and they've added that figure to their total retirement investment. They will now spend the afternoon working on a plan to make their retirement savings last as long as they do as part of an income plan that will support the future lifestyle of their dreams.

It's almost lunchtime. It's been a productive morning, and you've worked hard. Take a break, grab a bite, then come back ready to do some serious income planning. We've got time. The Ohio State game is a late afternoon start, the 3:30 national spot. We'll have some work to do before kickoff, and there will be things you and your spouse can talk about during the game. (The Buckeyes are playing Northwestern. If it was Michigan, we'd let you concentrate more.)

CHAPTER 3

Saturday Afternoon: Income Planning

Welcome back from lunch. What did you have? Are you ready to get back to work on a project that, when completed, will give you a better view yet of what your retirement years could look like from a financial standpoint?

We'll now begin the process of planning for ways to help get reliable retirement income, for a dependable monthly cash flow that will replace the regular paycheck you will no longer receive. This steady stream of income not only must pay for all your regular recurring monthly living expenses, but also for the "known unknowns" that pop up routinely in life. Moreover, this income plan must be adjustable to help address the effects of inflation, increased medical costs, and rising taxes. And most important, it must provide income you know will be there for as long as you need it.

Yeah, it's an important step, perhaps the biggest you'll take in deciding whether you are able to retire now or at some point in the future. So, let's get started.

Determine "mailbox income"

We begin the process by first determining what you can expect to receive in what many people call "fixed income." In a time before direct deposit, people once called this "mailbox income" as monthly checks were routinely delivered via the Postal Service. (We rather like the old-school term and will probably use it frequently in this section.)

This afternoon, we'll be addressing the income you know you will receive every month from Social Security, pensions or annuity payments, reliable rental incomes, regular dividends, interest, and possible employment. Yes, you read that correctly: possible employment. Employment has a place in retirement, but it should be only on your terms. We'll explore that idea more shortly.

If you haven't already, now is a great time to go online to the Social Security Administration website (www.ssa.gov) and determine what you will be receiving in monthly benefits from the system you've been paying withholding taxes into for as long as you've been employed. On the site, you can enter your personal information into a secure calculator that will give you the most up-to-date estimate on the monthly benefit you will receive.

Let's pause briefly and take this opportunity to comment on one of the essential basics of Social Security, something not completely understood by everyone preparing for retirement: Full Retirement Age (FRA).

The full monthly benefit to which you are entitled, based on your work history and what you've paid into the Social Security system, is due at your FRA. This age is a sliding scale as demonstrated in the chart below.

FULL RETIREMENT AGE

Year of Birth	FRA
1943-1954	66
1955	66 and 2 months
1956	66 and 4 months
1957	66 and 6 months
1958	66 and 8 months
1959	66 and 10 months
1960 and later	67

You are eligible to begin taking benefits as early as age sixty-two, but benefits taken before FRA are **reduced** by 6 percent (or slightly more) for each full year between start-up and FRA. In addition, the benefit you establish when first taking Social Security sets a *lifetime baseline,* not only for your benefit, but also for a spouse who can receive benefits despite not having a qualifying work history of their own. On a more positive note, a monthly benefit can be *increased* by 8 percent for each full year in which start-up is delayed until after FRA. These "delayed retirement credits" end at age seventy.

Tom, who was born in December 1959, already knew that his FRA was age sixty-six-and-ten-months. His visit to the SSA website today also told him that his monthly benefit at FRA would be $3,230.

But here in the spring of 2024, the sixty-four-year-old Tom doesn't believe he can wait until October of 2026 (his FRA date) to retire. After he and Jeannie spent the morning calculating their total retirement savings amount – the $1.7 million figure that stunned them – Tom set a goal for retiring on or shortly after his sixty-fifth birthday. He will become eligible for Medicare then, he figures, and won't have to worry about providing basic health insurance for himself if he can just hold on for a few more months. He also learns from his SSA visit that retiring twenty-two months before his FRA will mean he will receive only 87.8 percent of his scheduled FRA benefit. If he begins taking his monthly benefit at age sixty-five, it will be reduced to $2,836, a figure he and Jeannie think they can live with.

Jeannie, on the other hand, didn't have to consult the SSA.

As noted in the previous chapter, Jeannie already knows that she will receive a pension from Ohio's State Teacher Retirement System (STRS) in lieu of a Social Security benefit. And she knows (because she recently checked) that if she retires at her current age (sixty-two) that her monthly pension will be $3,500 if taken on a "life-only" basis. That payment will be reduced to $3,000 if the payout is guaranteed for the lifetime of both Jeannie and Tom.

The couple talks it over. Jeannie decides to pursue a "life-and-survivor" payout that allows Tom to continue receiving her pension should she pre-decease him. (In a "life-only" payout, her pension payments end at the time of her passing.) The higher-paying life-only payout option remains on the table, however, as an added income option should they decide they need it.

Tom and Jeannie have no other sources of "mailbox income." They have no other investments, having put everything into Tom's 401(k) and

Jeannie's 403(b). Their rental property hasn't been producing what they would call "reliable" income during the pandemic years, prompting their decision to sell it and use the proceeds as a future income source.

Until this time, our couple computes that, tapping into all their sources, they will have $5,835 in reliable monthly income – a figure they can adjust upwards should they deem it necessary to do so.

Let's look at what goes into this decision.

Estimate your anticipated retirement expenses

Nobody likes preparing a household budget. The process is only slightly less tedious than doing taxes, and we're not talking short form here.

Still, there are various times in life when you simply must take a closer look and compare the income you are receiving to the expenses you regularly incur, including the time just before entering retirement.

This doesn't have to be a completely unpleasant experience. Look, you just did half the assignment in calculating what you can expect each month in "fixed income." Estimating what you might spend in that same period is something a couple can do over the dinner table or even while watching TV. (If the program isn't, you know, commanding your complete concentration. You wouldn't want to try this during *Westworld* or *Breaking Bad*.)

Jeannie and Tom feel comfortable making approximate but informed estimates while watching Saturday afternoon's Ohio State game. Those dreadfully long TV timeouts and halftime provide plenty of opportunity to rough out routine monthly expenses, and then add in some more for non-routine expenses.

The list should be comprehensive, but most items will pop into mind quickly. Between the two spouses, someone will have a rough idea of what is spent each month on regular expenses such as groceries, utilities (including Internet costs and cell phone bills), fuel, mortgage or rental payments, car payments, life/casualty/health insurance, property taxes, entertainment/dining out, club or HOA dues, travel/commuting, and any other recurring expenses. Whew!

HOW TO RETIRE IN A WEEKEND | 19

And we're not done. Don't forget to account for non-recurring expenses that inevitably rear their costly head. An expensive auto or home repair, a short-term medical/dental expense, gifts you lavish shamelessly on your grandkids. We're sure you can think of others.

Another important consideration at this point: Don't short-change yourself when estimating your retirement expenses.

To be sure, you want to guard against overspending – you can't live a Dom Perignon lifestyle on a Bud Light budget – but don't be afraid to dream a bit in retirement. You've earned the right to some of the frills in life. Have a meal at Skyline Chili if you enjoy it, but don't be reluctant to have an occasional night on the town at the Pine Club, the Oakwood Club, Salar, or any of our other upscale restaurants in the Dayton area.

Tom and Jeannine, for instance, included in their "routine expense" list some things that don't appear on a recurring budget. Things like their frequent trips to visit their daughter and her three active pre-teens in Cincinnati, less than a one-hour drive in weekend traffic. They also budgeted for season tickets for the touring Broadway season at the Victoria Theatre, as well as Tom's desire to renew his season tickets for the Bengals. (He gave them up years ago but found a new interest about the time young quarterback Joe Burrow joined the team. Imagine that.)

When they were done counting sometime early in the third quarter of a Buckeyes' blowout win, Tom and Jeannie "guesstimated" they had roughly $8,000 in regular monthly expenses.

Then, they decided to go one step further. Actually, a couple miles further.

Tom and Jeannie have a bucket list of things they'd like to do now that they'll have the time to do them. These are things they hope to do early in retirement while they still have the physical ability to enjoy them during the "go-go" years of retirement. Their expense needs will likely turn to other areas during the "slow-go" and eventual "no-go" years that lie ahead.

They both are golfers who make an annual trip to The Memorial, the PGA Tour stop at Jack Nicklaus' Muirfield course near Columbus. But Tom has always dreamed of playing the original Muirfield in Scotland, as well as several other historical courses he's only viewed from the TV coverage of the British Open. Jeannie also would like to visit some of the places she's only described to her students in geography class. And both talk of spending more than a couple weeks each year with their son and his two kids at their home in Charleston, South Carolina. A couple of months nearby Myrtle Beach sounds nicer each year as the harsh Ohio winters suddenly seem colder to our retirement-age couple.

So, they add a $24,000 annual component to their "dream budget," a projected $2,000 additional monthly expense that puts their projected monthly "top-end" expense number at $10,000.

Clearly, their approximate $5,835 in mailbox income isn't going to cover their expense targets at either the low- or high-end estimates. Let's look now at ways that might help fill this deficit.

Fill the income gap

The difference between the money you expect to have coming in and what you believe will be going out is called your "income gap." It's a gap you don't want to have when actively employed, but one you might well expect when your self-provided "paycheck" is reduced in retirement while your living expenses remain much the same.

The challenge now is to fill this gap.

In our rough but informed calculations, the gap on the low side of the hypothetical couple's budget is $2,200 a month ($8,000 minus $5,800). This number can be filled rather easily from assets in their retirement savings.

The bigger challenge comes when filling a $4,200 gap ($10,000 minus $5,800) in their top-end "dream budget." We will set out to do so with the couple however, due to our belief that people should have the retirement of their reasonable dreams.

The important question now becomes, how much can the couple take each month from their $1.7 million retirement savings without being in risk of running out of money? Keep in mind that we're working to develop a comprehensive income plan that spells out in written detail how income will be provided not just for the first few years of retirement, but for a period that could span that twenty, twenty-five, thirty or more years.

There once was a staple of the financial services industry that said a person or couple could withdraw 4 percent of their retirement savings annually, adjust that number each year for inflation, and still have a high statistical probability of having enough savings to last through the course of normal retirement.

If this belief is accurate, Tom and Jeannie could consider taking a 4 percent annual drawdown from their $1.7 million in retirement savings and generate $68,000 annually, or $5,666 a month. That would appear to be more than enough to cover their $4,100 income gap on their top-end budget target.

But not everything is exactly as it appears. Let's explain why:

First, there's a reason we said the 4 percent drawdown rule was "once" considered all but sacred among retirement planners. There are multiple elements of the principle that are bothersome in the economic climate of 2022 when this book was originally written. Our concerns persist even in late 2023 as we were updating this book.

When the 4 percent rule was first theorized in the early 1990s, it was based on a reasonable expectation that a portfolio with a mix of stocks and bonds – say, a sixty/forty mix – would find one side coming to the support of the other during times of market downturns. In other words, when stocks were struggling, bonds would pick up the slack, and vice versa.

Well, bonds today are performing nowhere close to the way they did thirty years ago. Amid the low-performing nature of the bond market in 2022, many retirement planners today are urging clients to consider no more than a 3 percent drawdown from investment accounts.

How might this work for Tom and Jeannie?

Well, a 3 percent draw from their retirement savings would produce only $51,000 annually, or $4,250 a month. This would seem to fill, just barely, their $4,100 income gap.

Except that it doesn't.

The above math, you must understand, doesn't calculate the impact of taxes on the money the couple will be taking from their retirement savings.

It's important to keep in mind, but easy to overlook, that Tom and Jeannie both invested exclusively in tax-deferred retirement accounts – "qualified accounts" in IRS jargon. This isn't a criticism; it's the way most of us were taught to invest during our working years. The money we invested was done on a pre-tax basis. We got an immediate tax break, and our contributions were allowed to grow tax-deferred until the time the money was withdrawn.

That time is coming soon for Tom and Jeannie. And when it does, they will find that what they see on the bottom line of their account statements isn't all theirs to keep. Not after Uncle Sam finally takes his cut.

Let's now do some new math with taxes figured into the equation.

Same income gap, same total in tax-deferred retirement savings. A 3 percent withdrawal from a $1.7 million total is still $51,000, but now Uncle Sam and the state of Ohio have their hands out. As the couple hopes to live on around $120,000 annually, they were likely in the 22 percent federal tax bracket for 2024, and Ohio will likely demand an additional 3 percent. If the two taxing bodies take a combined 25 percent cut of their $51,000 withdrawal[2], Tom and Jeannie will net only $38,250 a year, or $3,187 a month. That can fill their income gap on their lower target, but not on the dream one.

So, what is the couple to do if they want to live the retirement of their dreams?

Consider adjustments to income plan

The initial calculation may be disappointing, but it doesn't have to stay that way. At Russell Total Wealth and Wellness, we routinely work with clients to make income plan adjustments that can help make a positive change in their retirement lifestyle.

An opening approach involves exploring new or expanded sources of income. Maybe you need to increase your current contributions to your 401(k) or IRA during the time you remain employed. Maybe you need to delay starting Social Security to permanently increase your monthly benefit. Maybe you need to continue working a few years longer than you'd hoped.

---

[2] Tax rates in America are progressive so only income beyond $44,725 is taxed at the 22% rate, but we are using a flat 22% for simplicity in this example. Effective tax rates will vary by each individual's situation.

Maybe you need to scale back the spending you hope to be doing once you are responsible for providing your own paycheck. But let's consider that our last resort for now.

And maybe, just maybe, you might consider employment during retirement. Think about it.

Employment during retirement doesn't have to be as distressing as it sounds, not if done for the right reasons. In the ideal scenario, you **choose** to work; you are not **forced** to do so to make ends meet. A chance to continue being around people, especially those you enjoy, is a good thing, and it's made even better knowing you can walk away at any time. And hey, having some extra income in retirement isn't a bad deal either.

If you want to ease into retirement – many do – you might choose to work part-time for a former employer who values your expertise. Or, you might consider trying something completely new and challenging, a kind of reset in life. A business owner who spent years growing a company might find it hard initially to scale back a once-hectic work schedule, but they might find comfort in the transition by continuing to maintain a presence, albeit a reduced one, around the shop. A teacher such as Jeannie might find she misses the kids – but not the nightly lesson plans – and continue to work in nearby schools as a substitute. (She might end up with more work than she wants, but she'll learn to say "no" when she's had enough.)

There are other ways to create new or potentially even more lucrative income streams that don't involve employment.

Jeannie, for instance, could consider expanding her monthly pension payment by $500 by electing the "life-only" payout option that does not offer payments to Tom should he survive her. Tom might consider rolling over his 401(k) into a self-controlled IRA that gives him more investment options and overall control of his own money. He might also delay taking his Social Security benefit later than planned at age sixty-five, an option should Jeannie consider working longer than he does. The two at some point should consider a way to turn the sale of the rental home into an income stream.

(We have multiple income-enhancement options to consider, including annuities that guarantee monthly payments for life while offering protection against loss of principal due to market conditions.

We may also look into a dividend-producing stock as an option, among other possibilities depending on your financial situation.)

But these are thoughts for another time.

Where has the time gone? Late afternoon has turned to early evening. The Scarlet and Gray have put another one in the win column, and it's time to take a dinner break, maybe an extended one. There are other things that will come to mind this evening and on Sunday. We'll consider them soon.

For now, Tom and Jeannie are feeling pretty good about what they've accomplished. They've done some real planning. They put pencil to paper and proved to themselves that their future retirement income can meet their retirement needs, and even some of their retirement dreams. They like the picture they've developed for themselves but know they still have some work to do.

They will take whatever time is necessary to get the job done. This whole process, they understand, is ultimately about creating future time for themselves.

CHAPTER 4

Saturday Evening: What's the Risk?

It's Saturday evening, shortly after dinner. Tom and Jeannie have had a full, productive day of planning. They deserve to feel good about all they've accomplished.

They've now got a good idea of what they've saved for retirement. They've also estimated how much they can expect to receive in monthly, "fixed" income, as well as how much they might spend on both regular and irregular monthly expenses. They know how they'll fill the gap between what comes in and what goes out. They proved to themselves that they have the resources that will help provide them a comfortable income over the course of their retirement, however long a period that might be.

And now they need some time to relax, each in their own way.

For Tom, it's watching the Columbus Blue Jackets in an early-season NHL game. Jeannie sits in through at least the first period, feigning more interest than she actually has. (Tom knows the drill. He does much the same thing when "watching" all those figure skating competitions that Jeannie loves.) Eventually, she'll move from the family room to the den where she'll pick up where she left off with a book or resume binge-watching something on Netflix.

As the TV plays in the background, both are thinking to themselves.

They realize now that they've done a better job than they ever thought possible saving for retirement. Their retirement nest egg is a nice pile of money, yet they still realize that these assets must survive for as long as they do. To be sure, they plan to continue growing these assets even as they begin drawing from them. In theory, they'd like this future growth to at least match (if not exceed) whatever they take out for income. In a worst-case scenario, they want growth that at least keeps pace with inflation.

This is an achievable goal, but often a challenge. Especially while dealing with market downturns like those of the first eight months of 2022 and 2023.

Tom and Jeannie aren't what you'd call "market watchers," but they are well informed people. Tom got spoofed in the summer of 2022 when the post-pandemic recovery contributed to a tidal surge of inflation – a 9.1 percent year-over-year increase in June that represented a forty-year high. Inflation, coupled with rising interest rates intended to curb rising prices, helped precipitate a bear market (a 20 percent decline) in both the Nasdaq and (briefly) in the S&P 500, as well as a significant correction (a decline of 10 percent or more) in the Dow Industrial Average when the year's first half ended on June 30, 2022.

Tom, you should know, doesn't spoof easily. When it comes to market volatility, he's been there and done that.

He was only a young investor then, but he still has fading memories of "Black Monday," the day in 1987 when the Dow tumbled nearly 22 percent *in one day*. Regardless, Tom continued to make regular contributions to his 401(k) and was rewarded during the market's 1990s go-go days. That period came to a crashing halt during the "dot-com bubble burst" when the tech-heavy Nasdaq fell some 78 percent from March 2001 through early October 2002. Just a few years later, the sub-prime mortgage crisis fueled the Great Recession during which the Dow lost 54 percent of its value from its high in October 2007 to its low in March 2009. It would be four years before the Dow again reached its previous high.[3]

Through these fluctuations, Tom held the line. He, as well as Jeannie, continued making regular contributions to their tax-deferred defined contribution programs, and were rewarded by a bull market that lasted through much of the second decade of the current century.

Until, that is, the inflation-driven market tumble of 2022 took out the bull's legs.

---

[3] Matthew DiLallo. Motley Fool. May 2, 2022. "The Biggest Stock Market Crashes in History." https://www.fool.com/investing/stock-market/basics/crashes

This time, the market tumble felt different, almost personal, to Tom and Jeannie. Unlike the two previous bear markets of the 21st century when the couple told themselves (accurately) that they still had time to recover from losses to their investment portfolio, time was no longer on their side in 2022. Not when they were now facing the imminent prospect of having to use their retirement savings – to the tune of some $4,100 a month – to supplement their regular retirement income. Now their decline in portfolio value becomes more than a "paper loss," especially when that paper is now the actual green stock upon which U.S. currency is printed.

Tom and Jeannie, who once told themselves they never again wanted to experience anything like the bear markets of 2002 and 2008, now realize they can no longer *afford* to ride out such downturns. So, during "Zamboni time," the break between the first two periods of the hockey game, Jeannie asks the question both have been thinking about for the past hour.

"You know," Jeannie began, turning to Tom, "that's a big pile of money we've saved. How much of it is at risk in the stock market? How much can be called safe?"

Take a hard look at your risk exposure

Good questions, ones they both want answered. Still, those answers likely won't be determined by the end of the evening, or even by the end of the weekend. It's something they'll set out to address in the upcoming week.

Both these questions are of a kind we hear often at Russell Total Wealth and Wellness where we routinely help people determine the risk level of their current portfolio and the personal level of risk tolerance with which they are comfortable.

Tom and Jeannie do have an advisor, one Jeannie contacted when first establishing her 403(b). The two women talked then about investments to be made within the account and the risk levels that Jeannie, who was in her early 30s at the time, would be comfortable with. Tom, who receives little to no professional guidance from the institutional management team operating his company's 401(k), will often sit in on their yearly reviews and ask market-related questions of Jeannie's advisor, hoping to pick her brain for guidance regarding his account.

Jeannie likes her advisor who's helped her grow $200,000 in a 403(b) that will supplement her teacher's pension; however, it now occurs to her that the two haven't recently discussed Jeannie's changing risk tolerance, much less the market-risk level of her portfolio.

In one of their first meetings almost thirty years ago, Jeannie remembers being asked what kind of losses she might be willing to take in the hope of getting a higher return. She and Tom both agreed then, in an off-the-cuff analysis, that they could probably accept a 10 percent loss in portfolio value without losing any sleep.

Now in their sixties, both have a new perspective. They've just realized that they've put away some $1.7 million toward retirement, and a 10 percent loss in that value is $170,000. No way, they now say, could they afford to take that kind of loss.

Their change in mindset is certainly understandable. They're both preparing to walk away from a regular paycheck, and they suddenly realize they have only a finite sum to get them to the finish line. Their focus has been on growth all these years, but now the objective has changed. They've become very protective of that money they've spent their lifetime saving. Who can blame them?

Now that their tolerance for risk has diminished over time, it's also necessary to explore whether the risk involved in their investments matches their new risk acceptance level.

Jeannie, for instance, knows she still has some of the same mutual funds she invested in during her forties. She doesn't know how to quantify the risk level of those investments twenty years later, but she has a gut feeling that she's overexposed to the ever-shifting winds of the market. Tom has had a similar feeling for years, one that only intensified during the market turmoil of early 2022.

So, what is the couple to do in this illustration?

At Russell Total Wealth and Wellness, when we meet with folks, we look at their overall financial situation to see how we can help address these concerns. We do this by using an interview process and then incorporating computer software. With these steps, we can more accurately determine a client's current tolerance for risk, a level likely very different at age sixty-five than it was at thirty-five, forty-five, or even fifty-five. People of retirement age often tell us they are more interested in protecting the money they've spent a lifetime accumulating than they are in taking undo risk to grow it. We are eager to help such people adjust their investments to meet these changing needs.

The other part of our risk analysis process involves "stress testing" our clients' portfolios.

We essentially put all a client's investments on a treadmill, hook them up to an EKG machine, turn the speed up to twelve, and see how they perform when the heartbeat reaches 180. For those not into cardio analogies, this involves "back testing" a portfolio by looking at how it actually performed during real-life past situations, among them "worst-case scenarios" like the bear markets of 2001, 2008, and 2022. Though past performance is no guarantee of future results, such examinations can help shed some light on how a portfolio might perform during similar times of future market volatility.

We often encounter new clients, especially those who've been working with large "strip mall" companies, who have their money largely invested in mutual funds that are stock-market driven. They likely don't know how much risk they are taking, and when we test their investments, roughly eight of ten people find they are at more risk than they are willing to take.

It's only after we've defined a client's current risk tolerance and determined the amount of market risk in their portfolio that we can begin to build a plan for future growth of those assets at a risk level with which the client is comfortable.

But first, we need you to work with us.

Maybe it's time for a change

It occurs to Tom and Jeannie later that while they've had many discussions about growing wealth, the couple has spent little time – and consequently know very little – discussing how to strategically take income from their accounts. It's a common problem people of retirement age face as they transition from the ***accumulation*** to the ***distribution*** phase of life.

Saving for retirement involves more than just investing in stocks, bonds, mutual funds, and ETFs – the things many brokers and advisors for the national brand-name companies who advertise on TV are most eager to discuss. There is nothing wrong with that, mind you, as there is certainly a place for this kind of accumulation advisor in the accumulation years of your investment life.

But people of retirement age need to consider more than just investments. For people like Tom and Jeannie, the more important issues now become, "How do we go about receiving all this money we've saved? How do we turn these savings into guaranteed income streams? How can we be sure we won't run out of this money? What rules apply to withdrawing from our retirement plans?"

Addressing these questions requires more than just discussions of stock market performance and total returns.

Retirement is a time for a different approach. And while your accumulation advisor likely served a useful purpose, it's now time to consider calling in a qualified professional that focuses on distribution.

Specifically, you need a distribution advisor, someone who focuses on working with people in or near retirement. You need a steady hand who knows ways to help you avoid the pitfalls of retirement by helping people create durable, reliable income they can count on for the rest of their lives. You need someone who can do this as tax efficiently as possible to help you keep more of **your** money in **your** pocket. You need someone with experience that can help find ways to put some downside protection into a retirement-age investment portfolio. You need someone well versed on health care needs in retirement, as well as providing for loved ones when you are no longer here to do so.

You need someone to help you develop a customized retirement plan that is based on more than the mere hope that market performance will produce the kind of returns you will need to live on for the rest of your life. If you're only *hoping* that your income will be there, you are using the wrong strategy.

And maybe the wrong advisor.

Tom has been thinking about these things throughout the second period of the Jackets' game, he goes upstairs to visit with Jeannie before the teams return to the ice for the final period.

"I'm thinking," he says, "maybe it's time to consider a change."

Build your Fiscal House™

If you find that your advisor talks mainly about stocks and bonds and the growth in your portfolio, or if, like Tom and Jeannie, you want to start hearing more about turning your investments into income, we suggest you also consider a change. And we (respectfully) suggest that you consider us.

At our company, we've spent decades helping clients take strategic distributions from retirement assets, drawdowns that can help assure that they will have reliable income – the actual cash necessary to fund the retirement of their reasonable dreams – for as long as they need it.

We also spend a lot of time talking about helping people of retirement age continue to grow their assets – money that may be needed for future expenses such as increased health-care costs or nursing care – at a risk level with which they are comfortable. For some people, this means no risk at all. Others may be more comfortable taking more risk. We'll talk about meeting these different concerns here shortly.

We'll talk about building – or remodeling, if you've already built – an investment portfolio based on our trademarked Fiscal House™ management philosophy, a "model home" with three essential components:

- The Foundation is defined as money that you only lose if you choose. These investments provide principal protection, fixed rates, earnings opportunities based on index participation, and guaranteed lifetime income. These are usually bank or insurance company products, such as CDs, and fixed or fixed indexed annuities or life insurance.
- The Walls are investments with the potential to produce both income and growth with reduced exposure and lower correlation to market volatility.
- The Roof utilizes higher-risk investments designed for the continued long-term growth and tactical management of your retirement assets at a risk level with which you are comfortable.

Let's look more closely at each part of the building plan.

The Foundation

As the name suggests, the foundation is the base upon which everything else is built. The foundation is intended to be strong enough that no matter how damaging the financial "storm" is – even if it takes off your roof and knocks down your walls – the foundation will be there to rebuild on.

The foundation is comprised of financial vehicles that are not exposed to market risk. Cash in bank accounts or CDs can be considered an essential part of the foundation. But cash and CDs – while certainly protected against loss – typically offer limited growth potential. As alternatives, we like to include two types of annuities among our foundation investments.

Now, we know of some people who will immediately turn the page right after reading the word "annuities." Please don't do that.

We often, talk to clients about both fixed and fixed index annuities – insurance contracts that offer contractually guaranteed income, the potential for growth, and protection against loss of principal due to market volatility. These guarantees are backed by the claims-paying ability of the insurance companies that write the contracts.

With a fixed annuity, you invest money with an insurance company for a designated period or for life, depending on your objective for this money. The money grows at a fixed rate of interest, usually ranging somewhere between 2-6% depending on the current market conditions. You can choose to surrender the annuity once the surrender penalty period ends, our continue to grow your money. You also have the option to turn the money into a guaranteed income stream

A fixed index annuity offers potential growth through credited interest tied to an increase in a chosen market index (Dow Jones Industrial Average, S&P 500®, NASDAQ, etc.) to which the contract is linked. If the index increases over the contract year, the annutity holder may receive a percentage of that growth; as interest, subject to limits set by the company; however, if the market decreases, prior earnings and principal are protected from loss.

For example, if the S&P 500® were to grow 12 percent over a year, an annuity holder with a contract linked to that index with 50 percent participation would receive 6 percent of credited interest generated by that index growth. Any interest credited to the account resets its base amount annually to a level that will not be decreased by future market performance. In down years, you may not receive any interest but you also won't see the value of your annuity decrease (unless you have purchased additional features that involve an annual cost, which will continue to be deducted from the annuity value each year).

That last part is the beauty, and the foundational benefit, of the index annuity in our opinion.

This protection against loss is made possible because of a type of "tradeoff" offered in the annuity contract. In exchange for only limited interest, the insurance company guarantees the annuity holder will incur *no loss* in years when the index shows a negative return. In the case of the above example, should the S&P 500® fall 5 percent in a year – or even 38 percent, as happened in 2008[4] – the annuitant's contract value does not decrease from any previous reset level.

Income via annuity payments typically begins after a defined minimum accumulation period. Riders to the contract can be added that guarantee these payments for the life of an annuitant and a spouse, if so designated. A rider offers additional flexibility and can potentially increase income received from the annuity.

When we talk about building a strong foundation for our Fiscal House, we talk of doing so through contractual guarantees, such as those an insurance company puts behind its annuity contracts. This is why the fixed and index annuities can be a suitable part of this foundation.

The Walls

The walls of our Fiscal House™ are built for the purpose of lowering your exposure to market risk. We're looking here at investments that *are not* highly correlated to market performance, ones that zig when the market zags. Growth is not necessarily the top priority. Rather, the goal is to create durable income streams you can reliably and predictably count on without taking undo market risk.

---

[4] Macrotrends. 2024. "S&P 500 Index – 90 Year Historical Chart" S&P 500 Index - 90 Year Historical Chart | MacroTrends

In short, our walls – like any wall – will have some exposure to the occasionally harsh winds of the market but are designed to survive the worst of storms.

Some of the alternatives to traditional market investments include real estate – either actual property ownership or involvement with real estate professionals through a Real Estate Investment Trust (REIT) – preferred stock, secured debt, and dividend-paying blue-chip stocks, the kind that Warren Buffett might invest in.

You might notice we said nothing of bonds here. In another time, we certainly would have. But 2022 was not such a time.

The income-producing potential of bonds once made them a staple of any retirement investment portfolio. You've no doubt seen pie chart illustrations suggesting that a person at age forty should have a sixty/forty split of stocks to bonds in their investment portfolio. At age sixty, however, that balance shifts to forty/sixty with bonds now representing the biggest piece of the pie. Or so says "conventional wisdom."

This balance comes from the "prudent investor rule," also known as the "rule of 100." This rule suggests that you subtract your current age from 100 to determine how much of your investment portfolio should be exposed to market risk. A fifty-seven-year-old investor, in theory, might have 43 percent of their portfolio in stocks (or stock-related mutual funds and ETFs) with the remaining 57 percent in bonds or other "fixed income" investments.

While we still believe in the principle of the rule of 100, we also believe it's important to find an alternative to bonds in the investment equation. In fact, we'll go as far as to say that we believe bonds should probably have come with a warning sign in 2022 and 2023. Let's briefly explain that position:

Bonds, which include U.S. Treasuries, were the gold standard for many years when investors sought an alternative to the uncertainties of stocks. In years of higher interest rates, bonds produced an attractive, reliable rate of return during times when stock prices were in a downturn.

But interest rates began to decline in the early 2000s, then raced to rock bottom a few years later. To help American businesses and consumers spend our way out of the Great Recession of 2007 through

2009, the Federal Reserve lowered interest rates to well under 1 percent, and eventually to near 0 percent. Bonds simply stopped producing income as they once did, and the effect was particularly hard on seniors who had come to rely heavily on the interest produced by bonds and bank CDs.

The outlook for bonds became even more worrisome around 2021 during the recovery from the Covid pandemic.

Americans came out of quarantine ready to spend on goods and services that were suddenly in short supply because of pandemic-related business slowdowns/shutdowns and supply-chain breakdowns. That type of sudden spike is the classic formula for inflation. To slow the inevitable inflation, the Fed attempted to tighten the nation's money supply by raising interest rates. Bonds and bank deposits began to produce slightly more interest, but higher rates also generate falling bond prices.

(Why is that? Well, imagine that you own a bond that has a 2.25 percent yield. If you hold that bond to its maturity date, you will get back your initial investment in addition to the interest you've received throughout the time you held it. But now you suddenly need cash and decide to sell the bond prior to maturity. Interest rates have risen since your first bought it, and now a prospective buyer can get a newly issued bond with a 2.75 percent yield. Your lower-yielding bond isn't an attractive option, and you likely will have to offer that bond at a price well below what you paid for it.)

The challenge is to find investments that can produce durable income with less direct co-relation to the market.

Such investments are out there, but you must know where and what to look for. There is still a place in our "walls" for low-beta, dividend-producing stocks, particularly preferred stock that pays a slightly higher dividend than common stock. We also still believe in the income potential of some short-term corporate and municipal bonds. We might talk about senior secured debt, a kind of loan investment in which a company asset is offered as collateral to secure the debt it owes you, the lender. Real estate is a source of protection against inflation – rents and property values tend to rise as inflation does – and participation in a REIT allows an investor to share some of the profits earned by professional real estate managers.

We have other ideas on investments that can produce income and still offer some form of mitigation against market risk. We're more than happy to discuss them with both new and existing clients.

The Roof

As the last part of a house frame to be completed, our roof is comprised of investments that will be exposed to market risk, at whatever level you are comfortable, in the hope of producing a corresponding level of return.

Any money invested here should be other than what is needed immediately for regular expenses or to fill an income gap. Think of this as money you can afford to lose – though you hope not to – as opposed to the "foundation" money that you cannot afford to lose.

OK, we can hear you now. Why, you might be asking, would I want to expose **any** of my hard-earned retirement savings to unnecessary risk at this stage of my life? Fair question.

As an answer, we would note that while retirement is a notable milestone on our journey through life, it isn't necessarily the finish line some people think it to be. Life goes on and future expenses – likely for rising health care costs – will need to be funded. Medical bills and prescription drug costs, for example, can only be expected to increase as our bodies break down over time. The need to fund possible nursing care is also a major reason for seeking the continued growth of money that you don't need right now for essential income.

Definitely, some people of retirement age can tolerate **zero risk** with their life savings. This is fine, especially for those who have guaranteed income with principal protection and the prospect of limited growth through the "foundation" investments we outlined previously.

But there are other people, primarily those who know they have income streams that will carry them through retirement, who are perfectly content with continuing to "play the market." Maybe they've done so throughout their lives and are comfortable with "the game." Maybe they seek the development of legacy gifts for future generations of heirs or charitable causes.

Whatever the need or motivation, we work with people of all income levels and different degrees of risk tolerance to develop and manage a retirement investment portfolio that fits their specific situation in life.

These plans typically have two different styles of management: passive and active.

The passive style essentially says, "You probably can't beat the market, so just *be* it. Buy an index fund – say, a low-cost ETF based on the S&P 500® – and just ride the wave.

The active management style, also known as tactical, doesn't believe in sitting on your hands and not trying to mitigate risks during volatile times such as 2001, 2008, and 2022. "Why just watch the market drop 40 percent and not do anything?" a tactical money manager might ask. Again, a fair question.

At Russell Total Wealth and Wellness, we often encourage our clients to be active, to keep their finger on the pulse of the market and work with us. Typically, active money management within tactical models costs more in fees than passive investment models.

Now, please don't get the wrong idea from the above statement. Yes, we absolutely have a place, and a plan, for people who prefer a more passive approach and don't want to spend their retirement years watching the stock ticker scroll across the CNBC screen.

Yet we disagree with the approach of Susie Orman, among others, who in the troubled times of 2008 advised readers/viewers to not even read their account statements, to just throw them away and ride out the storm.

Well, we also believe that a blue sky typically follows a thunderstorm, but here in Ohio, we are exposed to enough damaging weather to know you must continually be alert to the approach of dangerous storms. How can you make good decisions, if you don't know what's going on around you?

We consequently encourage our clients to read their monthly or quarterly account statements and to call us whenever they see something that concerns them financially. They may well find that we call them first, such as we did in early 2022 when we moved many people from bonds into cash positions.

Keep in mind, too, that though we develop a blueprint and begin construction on your Fiscal House™, the job isn't over even after the last finishing nail has been driven. How many new-home constructions, notably custom-built projects, are completed without a dozen or so adjustments? So, too, will we do "remodeling" work on your Fiscal House™ when necessary.

There are also times, as we all know, when it's advisable to get out of the game and take a seat on the sideline to catch your breath. For those not into our sports metaphors, we're saying there is no point in taking undo risks when you don't have to.

But first you must determine what kind of risk is right for you at different stages of life. We look forward to helping people like you do exactly that.

CHAPTER 5

Saturday Night (Late): A Taxing Issue

It's now late Saturday. Tom dozed off early during the third period of the Jackets game but awoke in time to watch Columbus overcome a one-goal deficit and score the game-winning goal in the final ninty seconds.

He's now wired, pumped and wide awake as he catches the 11 p.m. local news. (Jeannie turned in much earlier. Her days of trying to stay awake for Saturday Night Live are long over.)

The newscast has its usual mix of disturbing national news, the network-material that local stations use to fill out weekend newscasts. Eastern Europe is still unsettled. Inflation remains high. Congress is still fighting over spending programs, and the national debt continues to rise, now close to $35 trillion[5]. (Tom can't even imagine putting that kind of debt on a credit card.)

The segment on America's rising national debt concludes with a brief discussion of how to reduce it. If America ever wants to get serious about doing so, the Harvard economist being interviewed says it must start by 1) cutting spending, 2) increasing taxes, or 3) implementing a combination of both.

As Tom has yet to see his government do much of anything to reduce spending, he's got a pretty good idea of which way the wind will blow on this issue.

---

[5] https://www.usdebtclock.org/ Accessed July 11, 2024.

Just as he begins to mentally grouse about the impending prospect of higher taxes, Tom is hit by another thought generated from the long day of income planning he and Jeannie just completed.

"You know," he says to himself, "almost all the income we'll take from our retirement savings to supplement what we don't receive in fixed income will be coming from tax-deferred accounts. That money we've been growing for years is now about to be taxed – almost every cent that we withdraw – as ordinary income."

There are other tax-related considerations to the $4,100 Tom and Jeannie expect to need each month to fill the gap between their "mailbox" income and their essential/discretionary needs. Sitting in the 22 percent tax bracket as of last year's tax filing, Tom now calculates that the couple may have to take out in excess of $4,900 a month to realize an after-tax net of the $4,100 they will require.

The issue suddenly has him tossing and turning as he tries to sleep. "This retirement tax bite," he tells himself, "is really going to hurt. How did it come to this?"

Taxes in retirement

Tom has reason to wonder. Didn't he and Jeannie do pretty much everything they were advised to do when saving for their retirement through – *Warning, IRS jargon ahead* – tax-deferred defined contribution plans, which the IRS also calls "qualified" retirement plans.

Tom, remember, invested throughout his working years in his company's 401(k) plan, going as far as to contribute the maximum allowable over the past twelve years. Jeannie, upon returning to teaching full-time when her kids were older, did the same (though on a more limited basis) with contributions to her 403(b). They have no other investments after deciding to commit everything to their work-related retirement plans.

They can't fault their efforts. They were, after all, only following the "conventional wisdom" of the time. They invested in themselves on a tax-deferred basis and got an immediate tax break in doing so. Moreover, they were told that when they finally began paying tax on this money – most likely at a time in retirement – they would likely have a reduced income and consequently be in a lower tax bracket.

What's not to like about that deal?

Well, it **was** a sweet thing, and many Americans of Tom and Jeannie's generation readily took part in it. There was, everyone understood, a tradeoff in that tax payments deferred now would come due later. But hey, who thinks ahead to something happening at age seventy-three when you're getting a tax break at age twenty-five, a time you need every penny you can keep while getting started in life and, perhaps, raising a young family?

Eventually, the time comes to pay the tax bill due on the back end of this sweet deal.

Tom and Jeannie now realize, as many Americans do when retirement approaches, that the bottom line on their qualified account statements is not really the bottom line. Not all of that saved money is theirs to keep, not after Uncle Sam comes calling for his share that he's politely delayed mentioning for all these years.

And then there's that prediction about expecting a reduced income and a lower tax bracket in retirement. Yeah, someone may want to take that one back.

Tom and Jeannie, you see, just spent the day working on a plan that will produce almost as much monthly income in retirement as they realized as fully employed workers. Good for them. Retirement is a time when you ***should*** plan to live a reasonable lifestyle of your choice, not one you must necessarily reduce because of a drop in income.

Now, they also must ask themselves this key question: If we plan to realize the same kind of income in retirement that we knew in our working years, shouldn't we also expect to spend the same amount in taxes?

OK, for the sake of fairness, let's point out here that Americans do get something of a tax break in retirement. Specifically, Social Security benefits are not taxed for some people, and are only partially taxed for everyone else. The chart below shows the percentage of benefits that are subject to tax depending on the "provisional income" of a single filer or couple filing jointly.[6]

SOCIAL SECURITY TAXATION

Filing Status	Provisional Income	Benefits Subject to Taxation
Single	Less than $25,000	No benefits taxable
Single	Between $25,000 and $34,000	Up to 50% of benefits taxable
Single	More than $34,000	Up to 85% of benefits taxable
Married filing jointly	Less than $32,000	No benefits taxable
Married filing jointly	Between $32,000 and $44,000	Up to 50% of benefits taxable
Married filing jointly	More than $44,000	Up to 85% of benefits taxable

However, because our couple did little to this point to build up either a tax-free or tax-favorable source of money, most of Tom and Jeannie's other retirement income will be fully taxable at their current tax rate. Jeannie's pension is fully taxable, as is most of the money they will withdraw from their qualified accounts. The good news is, they still have opportunities to change this picture by moving money from tax-deferred to tax-free accounts. We'll address this in more detail shortly.

For now, let's look at taxes that looms just ahead on the retirement horizon of most Americans.

---

[6] Provisional income is determined by adding adjusted gross income as reported on IRS Form 1040 to all tax-exempt income and one-half of Social Security benefits. Source: "Income Taxes and Your Social Security Benefit." www.ssa.gov

The effect of required minimum distributions (RMDs)

Our couple will soon learn more about the IRS rules that will require them to begin withdrawing money from their pool of previously untaxed savings beginning at age seventy-three. This money they must withdraw is fully taxable, and it must be taken whether they need or want it for income. RMDs, consequently, have the potential to elevate a retired individual or couple into a higher tax bracket than they knew during years of regular employment.

Because we believe in trying to educate our friends, clients, and readers, let's spend a few paragraphs explaining how RMDs are determined:

Your annual required minimum distribution is determined by a formula that divides the total amount of one's qualified funds from the previous year by a ***life expectancy factor*** determined by the IRS. This life expectancy factor, which is different than actual life expectancy, decreases each year. This, if you remember your grade school math, means the quotient of our equation – your actual RMD number – will likely increase (and generate more in taxes) each year as you get older.

Let's look at an example:

Say you have a total of $500,000 in all your qualified accounts at the end of 2023. This might include tax-deferred money in one or more IRA that you maintained in addition to your 401(k), 403(b), SEP (Simplified Employee Plan), TSP (Thrift Savings Plan), or other qualified accounts.

Let's now say you turn seventy-three in calendar year 2023 and must begin taking RMDs. You must withdraw $18,868, the result of dividing $500,000 by 25.6, the life-expectancy divisor at age seventy-two in the IRS Uniform Life Table (as of rules in place in 2022). For your first RMD only, you have until April 1 of the following year to withdraw the required funds. All subsequent RMDs must be taken by Dec. 31.

Let's look at the following year. You took $18,868 out of the account in 2023. Investment performance in a typical year – though probably not in 2022 – likely replaced some or all that money with new growth. So, let's say your balance at the end of 2023 was $501,500. Now at age seventy-four, your IRS divisor is only 25.5 and your RMD for 2024 is increased to $19,667. That number is most likely to increase even more in the following years.

Let's also note here that you really, really, really want to correctly determine your accurate RMD.

The IRS imposes a 25 percent penalty (prior to 2023 this penalty was 50 percent), on any RMD amount you failed to take. (It can be reduced to 10 percent if caught and corrected promptly). Let's note, too, that each financial services firm with which you have a qualified account is required to report the year-ending amount to you via Form 5498. Yet we occasionally hear of people with accounts scattered among different firms, and this can make the accounting of your qualified money total more difficult.

Some final notes: If you have multiple qualified IRA accounts, you do not need to take money from each. The IRS cares only that you meet your required number – and, of course, that you pay the taxes owed on that number. You can take the required distribution from any one IRA account or combination of accounts. However, 401(k) plans fit into the equation, too, since the IRS mandates that withdrawals be taken from those qualified retirement accounts (but not Roth IRAs). Also, each spouse in a couple filing jointly must take their own RMD based on the money in their individual qualified accounts. In other words, a couple cannot take one RMD based on the total account values of the two spouses.

Keep in mind, too, that the IRS will get this money from somebody, someday. It would prefer that you pay this obligation during your lifetime, but should you fail to completely do so before you leave us, it will collect from anyone who might inherit the untaxed balance of your IRA. In other words, you could end up passing your tax obligation on to loved ones unintentionally.

Inheritors once could pay any taxes owed over the course of their own lifetimes by taking smaller RMDs (and paying less in taxes) at their considerably younger ages. Under this structure, an inherited IRA had the potential to live on and grow long after its founder passed.

But the "stretch IRA" was eliminated by the SECURE Act of 2019 for most non-spouse beneficiaries. In its wake, only a spouse (and few non-spouse exceptions) can inherit an IRA and take distributions over the course of their lifetime, using their own age to determine RMDs. But all ***non-spousal*** inheritors who receive an IRA after Dec. 31, 2019 are now required to liquidate and pay all taxes on any inherited IRA within a ten-year period.

This ends today's RMD lesson, though we're always happy to work closely with clients needing more help.

For now, let's just say that Tom, like many people his age, is only now starting to realize he will have a new source of taxable income, one he'd forgotten to include when making estimates of retirement expenses. And make no doubt: taxes should definitely be included in your calculations about the money you will spend in retirement.

He finally drifts off to sleep early Sunday morning determined to address this situation sometime in the near future, preferably sooner than later.

Let's look at some options he might consider.

Fill up your tax-free resources

There are things people can do – though not necessarily over a weekend – to help reduce future tax consequences.

One option we might consider doing this involves building up tax-free resources, which for many Americans means making full use of the Roth IRA.

Many readers are familiar with the Roth concept, but let's define it quickly: A Roth IRA, as opposed to a traditional IRA, is funded by money that has already been taxed. Like the traditional IRA, this money has the potential to grow over time. But unlike the traditional IRA, Roth money is not taxed when withdrawn under certain conditions.[7] Moreover, Roth money is not subject to RMDs, and contributions can be made after age seventy-and-a-half, something that can't be done with a traditional IRA. Also, Roth money also can be passed to heirs without a tax obligation.

There are two ways to build up a Roth IRA: ***contributions*** and ***conversions***. Let's deal with contributions first.

---

[7] Distributions from a Roth IRA can be taken with incurring taxes if done after age fifty-nine-and-a-half, and if the Roth account has been established for at least five years. Source: "Types of Retirement Plans," www.irs.gov

Annual contributions to a Roth IRA are limited both in size and by the income of the person making the contribution. IRS rules in 2024 limit annual contributions to both a traditional and a Roth IRA to $7,000, with persons age fifty and older allowed an additional $1,000 "catchup" contribution.

A bigger challenge to some taxpayers involves the income limits that restrict the eligibility for making contributions to a Roth IRA.

In 2024, a single filer with a modified adjusted gross income (MAGI) of more than $161,000 is not allowed to make a direct Roth IRA contribution. The same restriction applies to a couple filing jointly with a MAGI over $240,000.

(Let's add here, just for educational purposes, that there is no income limit that restricts eligibility for *traditional* IRAs contributions. There are income limits, however, that affect tax deductibility. These income limits are reflective of whether you are also covered by a retirement plan at work. In 2024, a single filer (who is covered by a retirement plan at work) making under $77,000 in MAGI could deduct their entire traditional IRA contribution, up to the allowable limit. An individual making between $77,000 and $87,000 could deduct a reduced amount, but a single filer making more than $87,000 could not deduct a traditional IRA contribution from taxable income. [42]

The limits for a couple filing jointly (who are both covered by retirement plans at work) are under $123,000 (full deduction), between $123,000 and $143,000 (partial deduction), and more than $143,000 (no deduction).

Consider the Roth 401(k) option

Another way of making Roth contributions has been around only since 2006. We often find ourselves wishing it had arrived on the scene much sooner.

The Roth 401(k), like the traditional 401(k), takes your contributions directly from your paycheck. (An employer match also is a possibility, depending on the employer's desire to participate.) Unlike a traditional 401(k), contributions to a Roth 401(k) are made on an after-tax basis. As is the case with any Roth, money in a Roth 401(k) is not taxed when withdrawn.

Not all companies offer the Roth 401(k) option – they are more costly to administer – but their popularity has increased considerably during their short life. Fidelity Investments reported in 2023 that 80 percent of 401(k) plans also included a Roth 401(k) option.[8]

One of the beauties of the Roth 401(k), in our opinion, is its ability to allow workers of all income levels to move money into a Roth account. There is no income restriction on participation in a Roth 401(k), though there are limits on annual contributions that mirror those on a traditional 401(k).[9]

In 2024, an individual – or both spouses in a couple – can each contribute up to $23,000 annually to either a traditional or a Roth 401(k). People aged fifty and older can make an additional $7,500 catchup contribution for a $30,500 total. Contributions could be designated for either a traditional 401(k) or the Roth option. Or, they could be divided between the two.

We believe not nearly enough people are aware of this opportunity. Even though an increasing number of companies are offering the Roth 401(k), we'd estimate that about only 20 percent of the people we see take advantage of it, most preferring to instead get the immediate tax break from the traditional 401(k).

Frankly, we wish more people made more effort to build up Roth accounts that will provide a tax-free alternative in the RMD years of retirement. Tom and Jeannie might soon be wishing they had done so.

Tom, to his credit, did participate in a Roth 401(k) shortly after his company introduced the option some eight years ago. He arrived late to the party – he still liked the idea of getting a tax break on the money he was saving for his future – but for around two-and-a-half years now he's been topping out his 401(k) with after-tax Roth contributions. He now has about $60,000 of the $1.25 million in his 401(k) in Roth money.

---

[8] Matthew Cann, Keedra Carroll, Jeffrey W. Clark. Vanguard. July 2023. "How Americans use Roth contributions in DC plans" https://institutional.vanguard.com/content/dam/inst/iig-transformation/insights/pdf/how-americans-use-roth-contributions-in-dc-plans.pdf

[9] IRS. September 22, 2022. "Retirement Plans FAQs on Designated Roth Accounts." Internal Revenue Service. https://www.irs.gov/retirement-plans/retirement-plans-faqs-on-designated-roth-accounts

That's a nice start, but taking even a 4 percent drawdown from that money will produce only $200 monthly in tax-free money.

Tom, who wants to retire in a few months upon reaching age sixty-five, probably doesn't have a lot of options on the contribution side, other than continuing to make Roth 401(k) contributions for as long as he works. Better late than never, we always say.

Jeannie has more choices.

At age sixty-two, Jeannie plans to keep working for a while. That could be a long while or a short while depending on what she decides. While she is employed – as earned income is generally required to make Roth contributions – she should consider switching her contributions from tax-deferred contributions to her 403(b) to either a Roth 403(b) if available (they are somewhat rare) or, more likely, into her own self-controlled Roth IRA. The second option gives her more control over how her money can be invested, though is more limited in the amount she can contribute each year. (See above.)

The Roth IRA conversion

While the couple's options are limited with contributions, they are almost unlimited on when it comes to conversions.

Many readers are at least familiar with the concept of the Roth IRA conversion. In short, it's the process of moving money out of tax-deferred accounts, paying the tax incurred on the withdrawal in the tax year of the move, and then moving that money into a Roth IRA where it can grow and later be withdrawn tax-free.

It's important to note here that there are no limits on the size of a Roth IRA conversion. A practical limit, however, is the amount of tax one incurs on the conversion and what this additional taxable income might mean to one's tax bracket. Consequently, many people do Roth conversions in bits and pieces over time to help avoid a huge tax bill. It's a most reasonable approach.[10]

Tom and Jeannie, we would suggest, are prime candidates to consider Roth conversions.

They are both still relatively young seniors at sixty-four and sixty-two. They have several years before RMDs kick in at age seventy-three. This is important as Roth conversions are not allowed after RMDs begin. (You'll be taking money out of qualified accounts then, but you can no longer reinvest it directly into a tax-free Roth.) They both have time to make gradual conversions at opportune times, those being when the additional taxable income will not elevate them into a higher tax bracket.

We routinely help people make strategic decisions on Roth conversions at Russell Total Wealth and Wellness – often with the help of a tax professional. We welcome the opportunity to discuss the option with you.

Pay me now or pay me later

There is one other consideration, a timing factor that Americans facing impending RMDs should consider when debating whether (or when) to do Roth conversions.

To put it most simply, taxes are historically low as of the writing of this book, , .and they might stay there for another two tax years.

No, we haven't lost our minds. The Tax Cut and Jobs Act of 2017, more commonly branded the Trump tax cuts, reduced marginal tax rates to some of the lowest levels in the past forty years. The chart below illustrates the differences between tax brackets in effect in 2017 (before the cuts became effective in 2018) and the adjusted rates of 2024.

---

[10] Converting an employer plan account to a Roth IRA is a taxable event. Increased taxable income from the Roth IRA conversion may have several consequences including (but not limited to) a need for additional tax withholding or estimated tax payments, the loss of certain tax deductions and credits, and higher taxes on Social Security benefits and higher Medicare premiums. Be sure to consult with a qualified tax advisor before making any decisions regarding your IRA.

COMPARING 2017 TO 2024 RATES[11]

Single Filer			
2017		2024	
10%	$0-$9,325	10%	$0-$11,600
15%	$9,326-$37,950	12%	$11,600-$47,150
25%	$37,951-$91,900	22%	$47,150-$100,525
28%	$91,901-$191,650	24%	$100,525-$191,950
33%	$191,651-$416,700	32%	$191,950-$243,725
35%	$416,701-$418,400	35%	$243,725-$609,350
39.6%	Over $418,400	37%	Over $609,350

Married Filing Jointly			
2017		2024	
10%	$0-$18,650	10%	$0-$23,200
15%	$18,651-$75,900	12%	$23,200-$94,300
25%	$75,901-$153,100	22%	$94,300-$201,050
28%	$153,101-$233,350	24%	$201,050-$383,900
33%	$233,351-$416,700	32%	$383,900-$487,450
35%	$416,701-$470,700	35%	$487,450-$731,200
39.6%	Over $470,700	37%	Over $731,200

It's important to note here that these brackets are legislatively scheduled to "sunset" at the end of 2025. Naturally, a change in administration or Congressional makeup before then might prompt an extension of these reduced brackets. It's also possible that a president or Congress of a different mindset might curtail the bracket reductions before their scheduled termination date.

But why gamble on legislative action?

The point to be made here is if you've got to pay tax on your qualified money eventually – which you'll have to do beginning at age seventy-three – why not do it now in the two-year window when tax rates are known to be lower? In a "pay me now or pay me later" world, you are well advised to pay at least part, if not all, of your bill at a time when you know the rate is lower than it is likely to be several years from now.

---

[11] Alex Durante. Tax Foundation. November 9, 2023. "2024 Tax Brackets." https://taxfoundation.org/2024-tax-brackets/

We would also encourage people such as Tom – now that he's passed the fifty-nine-and-a-half age at which he can withdraw IRA money without a penalty – to start thinking about eventually doing a rollover from his 401(k) into a self-directed IRA, a move he should consider at the time of his retirement or shortly after. The rollover incurs no penalty but gives the investor more investment options – unlimited options, really – that are not routinely offered in a company plan. Moreover, this person is now free to make IRA conversions at their own pace now that they are free of company restrictions on the movement of invested money.

No doubt, Tom and Jeannie will have a lot to think about when they finally get serious about talking – hopefully sometime soon – about their future tax structure with a financial advisor. This is part of what we do at Russell Total Wealth and Wellness. We meet with clients to help give them some ideas about tax-efficient strategies they might employ. We hope you might even consider contacting us.

CHAPTER 6

Sunday Morning: Estate & Legacy Planning

Tom and Jeannie are both feeling a bit spiritual as they return home from Sunday morning church services.

They've just heard their pastor talk about being thankful for the gift of life, a known blessing with an unknown shelf life. They've always understood this, of course, but never spent a lot of time thinking too deeply about the unpleasant but inevitable topic of their own mortality.

But today, at ages sixty-four and sixty-two, Tom and Jeannie who have spent the previous day doing some intense retirement planning begin to think about what life will be like for their loved ones when they are no longer here.

They don't say much, but each is thinking to themselves.

Tom's immediate thoughts turn to providing for Jeannie after he's gone. Jeannie, quite honestly, has entertained similar thoughts and concerns that border on worries. But she also thinks about how the couple has yet to establish a structured means of transferring their worldly assets to their two children and five grandchildren, the people they want to help most after they are no longer here. They've also discussed wanting to do something for their church that's been a big part of their lives and possibly something else for a regional charitable organization whose work with disabled kids they've long admired.

Admittedly, no one likes thinking about their own demise, but there comes a time when we all must plan for it. Our pre-retirement years are just such a time, a period when we start thinking not only about what we will do with the rest of our lives, but also what we will leave behind as our legacy.

Let's take a brief minute to define that somewhat esoteric term:

"Legacy" may mean something different to you than it does to your neighbor. A textbook definition would suggest that legacy is how we're remembered – "who tells you story?" as they sing in the finale of *Hamilton*. Legacy cannot be measured exclusively by how much money you leave behind but should also invoke memories of a life well-lived. How you prepare for the end of that life, and what you can do to make things a little easier for those who follow you, is a big part of your legacy.

This is why legacy planning is a principal component of our holistic retirement plan. This planning is something you will want to at least consider over the course of the weekend, then act on reasonably soon. It's why Tom and Jeannie, upon arriving home from church, finally agree to talk about some things previously left unspoken. They'll make time to do so in the hours between brunch and the 4:20 p.m. kickoff of the Bengals national TV game with division rival Baltimore. (Yes, even something as important as legacy planning must occasionally take a back seat to the NFL Game of the Week.)

Providing for a surviving spouse

Providing income for a surviving spouse should be part of any comprehensive retirement plan. One of the first steps in doing this involves exploring the "survivor benefits" of Social Security, something people can do through a visit to the agency's website (www.ssa.gov) or by continuing to read on in this section.

For most couples with both spouses actively receiving Social Security benefits, the survivor benefit is fairly cut and dried. The surviving spouse continues to receive the larger of the two benefits. The other benefit disappears. (There are other provisions for survivors with disabilities and those with minor children, but we'll deal exclusively with retirement-age issues here.)

The loss of one monthly Social Security check often requires some income adjustments for the survivor. Regular monthly income can also be reduced if the deceased was receiving a pension payable over their life only or was actively employed on a full or part-time basis.

But while the survivor's income is likely to be reduced, regular living expenses aren't likely to change appreciably. Housing costs – rent/mortgage payments, insurance, property taxes – will be about the same for one person as they were for two. Grocery costs may decline, and you will no longer pay for supplemental health insurance for the deceased. But regular utility costs – electricity, water, phone bills, internet – are not likely to change much. As a result, some adjustments to the survivor's income plan may be needed.

This is particularly likely in the case of Tom and Jeannie, who have a unique dilemma.

You may recall that Jeannie, a teacher covered by an Ohio state pension program, made no contributions during her working years to the Social Security trust fund. She consequently did not receive Social Security benefits and will likely receive little or nothing of Tom's benefit should he predecease her.

She will continue to receive her own pension as well as take drawdowns – fully taxable ones – from both her own 403(b) and the 401(k)/rollover IRA she will inherit from Tom. But as Tom's Social Security benefit accounted for roughly 30 percent of the couple's monthly income, Jeannie may well need to consider changes in her income plan. She need not live life as a pauper, but she may well have to look into reducing her spending and possibly finding an alternative source(s) of income.

Fortunately for Jeannie, she has some options.

The role of permanent life insurance

Shortly after the birth of their first child, Tom and Jeannie purchased a permanent life insurance policy on Tom, the family's primary wage earner. They spent what they could at the time on premiums ($100 each month), which they paid over a twenty-year period. By the time Tom was forty-seven, they had a paid-up policy with a $120,000 death benefit. The policy has been sitting idly since the premiums stopped. (The couple sometimes forget they even had it.)

But that death benefit will be appreciated by the time of Tom's passing. It will hardly leave Jeannie "set for life," but she at least has some additional financial support when she will need it most. This, after all, is the traditional role of life insurance.

But that "traditional role" has changed and expanded in the years since the couple last paid a life insurance premium.

To provide more information, let's offer a brief primer on what we see as some additional benefits of today's life insurance as a financial vehicle in retirement plans.

Yes, we use the term "financial vehicles" when talking about life insurance. We do so because permanent life insurance, as opposed to term insurance, is a long-term investment in which you leverage a smaller amount of money (the premiums you pay) into a bigger resource (a larger death benefit) over the course of time. Moreover, many of today's life insurance products offer long-term benefits for young seniors who purchase new policies or convert older policies into newer models.

OK, we can again hear what you might be thinking at this point.

There comes a time, usually after their children have grown and moved out of the house, when people question the need for life insurance. "Why do we need life insurance at this age?" they often ask. Even the idea of receiving an enhanced death benefit leaves some people cold. (Sorry, bad word choice.) The idea of providing for someone else through a death benefit may not mean much to, say, a lifelong bachelor or bachelorette.

But there are aspects of today's life insurance products that can be helpful for people from all walks of life. Let's look at a few.

For people with dependents, the idea of providing a source of income when you are no longer here to do so seems obvious. Let's also consider the IRS rules that allow an insurance policy's death benefit to be available to beneficiaries of all ages on a **tax-free basis**[12]. Compare that to the tax bite incurred by non-spousal inheritors of IRAs, as described in the previous chapter.

There is, in fact, on strategy that people who don't need the RMDs they are required to take on their qualified accounts can consider. It

---

[12] Life insurance death benefits are generally tax free to a properly named beneficiary. Life insurance agents do not provide tax or legal advice.

involves taking the RMDs, paying the taxes due, and then using a portion or all of the money to pay the premiums on a permanent life insurance policy. This strategy requires that a person be medically able to be underwritten for life insurance, but for these people, the excess payments above and beyond what's needed to pay for the cost of the life insurance can accumulate inside the policy. It has the opportunity to grow and may ultimately produce a tax-free benefit to someone – presumably someone(s) very dear to the insured[13].

One more aspect of this strategy: the beneficiary of this tax-free money might just be you, the insured.

Some of today's permanent life insurance policies feature what are known as **accelerated benefits** or **living benefits**. As the name implies, this allows the insured to use a part of the death benefit while still living. Some policies can generate tax-free income – *let's say that again,* **tax-free income** – through withdrawals or low-interest loans that can be taken on any built-up cash value in the policy. The insured has the option of replaying the loan, with interest, or not repaying it and reducing the death benefit.

Moreover, some life insurance policies today also have provisions that allow part of the death benefit to be used to fund long-term nursing care should it become necessary. This kind of means of paying for long-term care is provided by both life insurance and some annuity vehicles. We'll talk more about this in our next chapter on health care coverage in retirement.

After doing some Sunday afternoon research, Jeannie is feeling a bit better about her long-term financial life after Tom is no longer with her. (She doesn't want to think about the emotional aftermath just yet. Perfectly understandable.) She's also pretty sure Tom will be all right financially if she passes first.

But then another thought comes to mind. It's about the inheritance they hope to pass on to their kids and grandkids. They've still done nothing to assure an orderly passing of their assets to the loved ones they will leave behind.

---

[13] Life insurance policy loans and withdrawals will reduce policy death benefits and cash values, and could cause the policy to lapse or require additional premiums to keep it in force. This assumes the policy is not a modified endowment contract ("MEC").

Preparing an orderly transition of assets

There will come a time – and it may come sooner than later, though we hope this isn't the case in your situation – when you will need to assure the orderly transfer of your worldly assets to those you want to receive them when you are no longer here.

Many people put off doing this, and we understand why. No one likes to think about their own demise. But we also know that too many people wait until it's too late to do anything which can present tremendous problems.

Now is as good a time as any to begin the process of "putting your affairs in order," to make things as easy as possible for your heirs at the difficult time when they are mourning your passing. We've all heard horror stories told by grieving loved ones who, at one of the worst times of their lives following the death of a parent, find themselves pouring through desk drawers and storage boxes looking for insurance statements, bank accounts, property deeds, car registrations, a will, or other legal documents that become necessary during this transition phase of life.

It doesn't have to be that difficult for the people you care about most. Not if you begin planning while you still can.

There are three basic ways to transfer the assets of your estate – and everyone who owns anything has an estate, no matter how large or small – after your passing. We would define them as ***transfers, wills, and trusts***. These are purposely listed in the order of least to most effective, in our opinion.

Transfers: Simple, but few things in life are this simple

A *transfer* is a relatively simple process in which you sign a document that shifts ownership of an asset to a designated beneficiary at the time of your death.

People with limited assets – say, a renter whose only significant property is a car – can have their bank accounts transferred to one or more beneficiaries by signing a Pay on Death form (POD) at their local bank. Ownership of a car can be legally changed with a Transfer on Death form (TOD) available at your county courthouse or local Department of Motor Vehicles. Properly updated beneficiary designations will direct payments from insurance policies or annuities to the person(s) of your choice without securing the assistance of an attorney. Distributions of prized possessions or heirlooms can be done by simple agreement if you are sure there will be no disputes over who gets what.

Simple, right? But things in life are rarely that simple. They can get even more complicated after your death. That's why we're not big fans of the POD/TOD school of estate planning. And frankly, very few people we see on a daily basis – and likely even fewer readers of this book – have estates that can be settled this simply. More often than not, legal help is necessary.

A will is a way, but not the best one

A *will* is a legal document, often (but not always) drawn up by an attorney, that specifies how you want your assets distributed after your death. We consider a will to be the bare-bones requirement of an estate plan, but also regard it as little more than that.

Let's explain why.

Granted, having a will is better than having nothing at all. Dying without one is called being ***intestate***, which means a probate court must decide the distribution of your assets. This court-ordered final distribution may or may not be anything close to what you intended.

But even a legal will is subject to probate court approval. We sometimes refer to wills as an admission ticket to probate court, and we're not trying to be cute or funny in doing so. There's nothing cute or funny about probate court.

To be sure, some wills are certified in a relatively quick manner. This happens once the probate court has verified the validity of the will, ascertained that there are no challenges to it, and established that the will's executor has paid all claims and taxes owed through the proceeds of the estate.

That's the best-case scenario. Now consider the alternative.

Probate proceedings are a matter of public record, which means the estate of the late-great you is available to creditors and predators alike. Attorneys we know often tell stories of people who search obituaries for targets, then pour through courthouse records for information about the estate being probated. We occasionally hear stories about creditors who come out of the woodwork with claims that may or may not be legitimate. Frequently, relatives will fight about what was promised to whom, and such disputes are not always settled easily or inexpensively.

Sometimes even non-relatives get involved. More than one relative of a deceased family member has been stunned to hear someone they've never known tell the probate court, "I drank coffee with my late friend Joe every Friday for fifteen years, and he promised me the Corvette he was converting." Or words to that effect.

That type of thing should have no place in your estate planning, which should be a private endeavor. Our goal is to help protect the sanctity of the process, allowing you to share only as much as you feel comfortable sharing with the people you want to know.

Although using a will as a main means of distributing your estate is one way you could do this, this may not be the right strategy for your situation. We always recommend to our clients that they consult with an estate planning attorney to determine what is right for them.

. Among other possible problems, settling a will that is contested or subject to creditor demands can be long and costly. Ohio attorneys we work with tell us that court costs and attorney fees can routinely come to between 2 and 5 percent or more of the total estate being contested. That's far too high a price to pay for a process of settling financial affairs that should remain between you and the advisor you trusted to help you manage your assets.

The relative safety of a trust could be another option.

In trusts we trust

A ***trust*** is a collection of legal documents that controls the distribution of assets included in the trust. The originators (also called "grantors") of a revocable "living" trust have full control over all assets in the trust until the death of the originator (or both originators in a couple). Following the passing of all originators, control of the trust passes to a **successor trustee**, typically a family member, trusted friend, or sometimes the trust department of a bank or other financial institution.

A trust, like a will, contains instructions from the grantor(s) to the trustee for distribution of assets. A grantor(s) might order an equal distribution of assets to all surviving children, for instance, or can leave specific instructions regarding any particular beneficiary. Let's consider an example.

An originator parent concerned about an adult offspring who doesn't handle money well, or perhaps has a substance abuse problem – "They'll blow through this money in a year if we don't do something!" – might instruct the trustee to disperse their money differently from that given to a more responsible child. Distributions to grandchildren or other second generations heirs might be withheld until the age of majority. The grantor might also designate distributions to a church, charity, or school.

Unlike a will, however, a trust is not subject to approval by a probate court. A trust is not a public document, and its holdings are not open to a public scrutiny. A creditor can make claims against a trust, but this involves filing a lawsuit – a far more difficult process than just showing up in probate court and making a claim.

Note that there are two kinds of trusts: revocable and irrevocable. The first, the revocable living trust described above, can be changed at any time or revoked completely by its originator(s). Conversely, an irrevocable trust cannot be changed. These trusts are often used by people with considerable wealth as a way of protecting heirs from estate taxes. They also are sometimes used to shelter the assets of people hoping to qualify for Medicaid payments for long-term nursing care. (More on this in the upcoming chapter.)

A trust also routinely includes several other important legal documents, ones we urge clients to secure whether or not they opt to have a trust.

The power of the POA

Foremost among these are two separate power of attorney (POA) assignments, one dealing with routine business matters and the other with health care decisions. Should the person establishing the POA designations become physically incapable of making decisions, their designated representative can write checks, pay bills, and make essential health care decisions.

POA designations become invalid at the time of the originator's death, at which time the roles of an executor or trustee kick in.

Also included in most trusts is a "living will" directive, instructions regarding life-prolonging medical procedures that may or may not be used according to the wishes of the originator.

Let's acknowledge at this point that establishing a trust is slightly more expensive than establishing a will. There are, quite simply, more legal documents to prepare in a trust. But we would also argue that these "extra" documents – the two POA designations, the "living will," the HIPPA directives, the "pour through" will – are worth the added expense. We'd also suggest that the added cost of preparing POA designations is an expense you should consider even if not opting for a trust.

We say this because we've personally known of situations in which a one spouse, needing to access money from the other's IRA for their medical care, has been unable to do so. "IRA," remember, stands for "individual" retirement account. And while a spouse may be a beneficiary on the account, they are not an owner. Not yet anyway.

"We'd love to help you," one client heard from the company holding her husband's IRA. "But unfortunately, there's nothing we can do until he passes."

Having a POA designation, however, allows you to legally care for your loved ones as they lay incapacitated in a hospital with the medical bills piling up. It's sad to say it, but in today's litigious society, you need a legal document that says you can regardless of your marital status. And yet a lot of spouses don't realize this. They say, "We're married, we've been together forty-five years. What do you mean I can't access my husband's money to pay our bills?'

It's something a lot of people overlook, but it's a real situation. Money in a lot of retirement accounts is off the table until the incapacitated spouse dies. But a person holding the power of attorney for business matters – the concerned wife in this example – can access funds from, say, her husband's IRA. This is just one of the reasons we urge clients to work with an estate planning attorney to secure a POA assignment while a loved one still has the capacity to give it or, alternatively, consider establishing a trust that bestows POA authority.

Estate planning takes a team

It seems obvious but must be noted: We are not attorneys and do not prepare the legal documents required for comprehensive estate planning. Still, we work closely with several estate attorneys in this field of law whom we've come to know and trust.

Working with an estate planning attorney is important. Just as you wouldn't want your general practitioner to do your knee replacement surgery, you likely won't want a personal injury lawyer setting up the distribution of assets you spent a lifetime accumulating. There are elements of estate law that are difficult for the lay person to understand. Confession time: We don't understand all of it either, which is why we work closely with people who do.

We typically work together as a team, one that often features a third "special teams" player from the world of tax accounting, such as a CPA.

Each team member has responsibilities that ultimately mesh together. The estate attorney prepares the legal documents required. (A trust often requires a bulky three-ring binder to hold all the papers. We wonder whether anyone ever reads them all.) The advisor works with the attorney to help make sure all your assets are properly "titled" to your trust. This is essential, as assets not correctly "funded" to the trust are as protected as a dropped wallet. And the CPA is on call to help address the multitude of usually-confusing tax issues that come with transferring assets.

That last assignment is especially important. While we know a lot of lawyers who are skilled at handling DUIs, divorces, and disputes, we also know that not everyone is as skilled as they might be on tax law.

In regard to estate planning, a relatively simple "putting your affairs in order" exercise can and should be done without a lawyer's attention.

Reviewing and updating (if necessary) the beneficiary designations on your bank accounts, insurance policies, investments, and retirement accounts is one way of getting your assets into the hands of the people you love even if you don't, you know, get around to doing all the things we've just outlined. (It happens, we get it.)

Yet there's no reason why, during a routine annual review with your advisor, you can't take the brief time necessary to make sure your beneficiary designations reflect your current intentions. Things may have changed since you first listed who you want to receive your assets when you pass. Family situations change through — sad to say it — disputes, divorce, and even death. Special health or care needs may arise among your children or grandchildren.

Bottom line, even if a will or trust isn't appropriate for an individual or couple, a person can avoid a lot of problems by making sure their beneficiary assignments are accurate and updated.

And now it's lunch time, early Sunday afternoon. We've given you a lot to think about in the hours after church. And no, you're not going to develop an entire estate plan by the end of this weekend, not even if you can find an estate attorney who works on a Sunday. (As if!)

But you can set your mind on working soon to develop a plan for the inevitable time when you are gone. We hope that time is a long, long way down the road. But well before whenever "then" is, you can write the script for how you want your loved ones, or people and organizations that are important to you, to remember you after you're gone. You can take the steps necessary to write the final chapter of your own legacy.

Let's get on this sooner than later. But first, let's take some time between lunch and the Bengals' kickoff to think about something more immediate. That is, working to keep you around for as long as possible.

It's time to think about your health care in retirement.

CHAPTER 7

Sunday Afternoon: Affording Health Care & Long-Term Care

Tom and Jeannie are finishing up lunch. It's just shy of 1 p.m., a full three hours before the Bengals' kickoff.

Between bites, Jeannie talks to Tom about her after-church research into the time – hopefully, a time well into the future – that sadly will leave one of them living on without the other. Tom listens carefully, thinking about how he's glad his wife did this morbid research instead of him. He agrees that the two need to get serious about their estate planning sometime soon.

Jeannie isn't done prodding him.

"You know," she says, "you're talking about retiring after you turn sixty-five in a few months, and I've got no problem with that. You'll be eligible for Medicare then, and that's great. But what about me? I won't be covered by your group plan anymore, and I'm still three years short of 65."

What Jeannie has pointed out is common problem many Americans of retirement age encounter. We often visit with clients who say they will probably work a few years longer than they would like just to retain their employer's health insurance. We routinely work with such people to help find alternative considerations.

Tom and Jeannie set out to do their own research.

Jeannie returns to the computer in the den. She explores options for COBRA coverage, an eighteen-month period in which she can stay on her current plan by paying her own, admittedly higher monthly premiums. She'll also visit HealthCare.gov, the marketplace for federally subsidized health insurance created by the Affordable Care Act (ACA). She immediately feels a bit overwhelmed by all the options there.

She would like to retire at a time of her choosing but begins to think about insurance options available if she keeps working. She considers calling teacher friends to inquire about coverage they have through the STRS Ohio Health Care Program. If she was reading this book, she would learn of a Dayton-area company that puts together private group coverage policies that might interest her. (These policies can be hard to find, but we know where to look.)

She will discover multiple options, but all of them will incur an additional expense, another monthly drain on their income plan once Tom retires and tempts Jeannie to do the same.

Tom has his own approach to weekend research.

He settles down before the TV and checks the 1 p.m. football lineup. The CBS affiliate is offering Cleveland vs. Jacksonville. Ugh. The local Fox station is offering Chicago vs. Minnesota as its regional offering. Only slightly better.

Tom puts the Browns game on as background noise and fires up his tablet. He'll spend parts of the next three hours researching his Medicare options. He knows the basics – or at least as much as most Americans do – but is unsure about signup procedures, prescription drug coverage, and why he is continually bombarded by 10,000 TV ads, mail pamphlets, and the never-ending string of annoying phone calls promoting Medicare Advantage.

But you, dear reader, don't have to work that hard.

Here in the Twenty minutes it takes to read this chapter are most of the things our couple will learn during their three hours of internet research. Included, too – at no additional charge, of course – are some things they likely won't find out through only light browsing.

Health care expenses in retirement are a major drain on any retirement nest egg. In 2024, Fidelity Investments issued an often-quoted estimate that a married couple at age sixty-five can expect to spend more than $315,000 on out-of-pocket medical expenses over the course of an average retirement. This estimate includes insurance premiums, co-pays, deductibles, and other costs not covered by Medicare.[14]

Don't expect this estimate to go anywhere but up in the coming years. Our medical costs rise naturally as our bodies age, break down and require more attention. Medical expenses in our eighties will be greatly different than in our sixties.

Now consider the effect of inflation, which in June 2022 rose to 9.1 percent year-over-year – the biggest monthly increase in forty years. That spike validates the potential challenges inflation can pose, though the twelve-month rate dropped to 3 percent by June 2024, its lowest level in more than three years.[15]

And we haven't even begun to discuss yet the potentially budget-crippling costs of future long-term nursing care, which we'll do later in this chapter.

Clearly, securing the most complete health care coverage you can get is a major component of any retirement plan. That coverage for most Americans entering retirement age starts – but doesn't end – with Medicare.

Medicare basics: Learning your A, B, C, and Ds

The Medicare website (medicare.gov) is very helpful, but it also contains reams of material that would make even an accountant's eyes spin. So here, in as concise a manner as we can, are the essentials of Medicare.

Medicare, the government system of health care for people age sixty-five and older that began in 1965, consists of four parts, A through D.

---

[14] Fidelity. June 20, 2024. "Keys to covering health care in retirement" https://www.fidelity.com/learning-center/wealth-management-insights/how-to-prepare-for-health-care-costs-in-retirement#

[15] Jeff Cox. CNBC. July 11, 2024. "Inflation falls 0.1% in June from prior month, helping case for lower rates" https://www.cnbc.com/2024/07/11/cpi-inflation-report-june-2024.html

Parts A and B are considered "traditional" Medicare. Part C, also known as Medicare Advantage, is cost-controlled alternative coverage that includes all components of parts A and B, as well as some things not covered by "traditional" Medicare. Part D is prescription drug coverage, an optional add-on to traditional Medicare but is included in Advantage plans.

Let's look first at the costs and coverage of "traditional" Medicare. We'll deal with optional Parts C and D here shortly.

Part A: Hospital coverage

Part A covers hospital charges when you are an overnight patient whose admission was ordered by a physician. (Emergency rooms visits and outpatient surgeries are covered by Part B.) Charges for the use of a hospital's facility and staff are covered, but those of surgeons and other support personnel are not.

Part A covers charges on a hospital stay of up to sixty days once an annual deductible ($1,632 in 2024) is met. Stays of more than sixty days incur a co-insurance charge of $408 per day (again, in 2024). Part A also covers hospice, some home health care, and a *limited* stay in a skilled nursing facility. It does not, however, cover an extended stay in *custodial care* – a distinction that leads people to sometimes mistakenly believe that Medicare covers long-term nursing care. It doesn't.

The premium for Part A coverage is paid by most people through the Medicare tax that is withheld from regular paychecks. This 1.45 percent tax is paid by both the employee and the employer. People who did not pay this tax must pay the Part A premium out of pocket.

(This will present a significant problem for Jeannie, who as an Ohio teacher did not pay Social Security taxes during her teaching years. She soon learns from her research that people who do not have forty quarters of paying Social Security taxes will pay a monthly Part A out-of-pocket premium of $505. She also learns that a spouse of a fully-qualified worker can incur a reduced premium of $278 monthly. She hopes to fall into the second classification and puts this at the top of a to-do list of things to check later.)

Part B: Medical coverage

Part B covers most (but not all) out-patient charges from medical providers. Covered costs include those from physicians, laboratories, radiologists, preventative and diagnostic services, ambulance calls and emergency room visits (in the event of sudden illness or injury), mental health services, limited home health care, and rehabilitation equipment.

But Part B generally covers only about 80 percent of the above costs. The remaining 20 percent is the patient's responsibility, and that share can be considerable in the aftermath of a major surgery or extended illness. Covering this difference is the role of Medicare supplement insurance, which we will discuss later in this chapter.

Part B is *not* premium-free coverage. A premium of $174.70 was withheld from the monthly Social Security benefit of Plan B participants in 2024. This premium is paid out of pocket by people not yet receiving Social Security as well as those who will never receive it. (Yet another potential retirement expense for our Jeannie.)

Technically, Part B is optional coverage, but you must take care if you choose to delay it. Here's why:

People (as well as their spouses) who are covered by what Medicare calls "creditable coverage" can opt out of Plan B for as long as that alternative coverage remains in effect. Creditable coverage, such as that provided by most employer-sponsored group plans, covers all Medicare does. A person covered by such a plan can apply for Medicare but opt out of paying the Part B premiums.

However, when the employer coverage ends – such as when you retire – a person has eight months during a special enrollment period in which to sign up for Part B. The failure to do so has significant consequences. Medicare will impose a 10 percent penalty on all future premiums for every twelve-month period in which you could have had Part B coverage but declined to take it. This penalty, mind you, will be paid on all future premiums for as long as you live.

We'll explore Medicare enrollment in more detail later in this chapter, but for now, let's continue with our Medicare basics.

Part C: Medicare Advantage

Medicare Part C, more commonly called Medicare Advantage, offers a lower-cost option to supplemental insurance policies that cover what Medicare does not.

Advantage policies are written by private insurance companies who essentially administer the Medicare program on behalf of the government. These companies, who are reimbursed by Medicare, attempt to control costs by contracting with a network of medical providers who agree to a fee schedule offered by the insurance company. Advantage plans are required to include all coverage offered by "traditional" Medicare. Most offer even more services through prescription drug coverage and limited vision, dental, and hearing examinations that are not covered by Medicare Parts A and B. Some plans even offer free enrollment in a fitness center.

The main selling point of Advantage plans, in our view, is their low costs when compared to Medicare supplemental coverage.

Some plans can be purchased for $0 while others can range as high as $327 per month. On average, the cost is $27 monthly.[16] All plans come with co-pays and deductibles, much like standard HMO or PPO plans. The zero- and lower-cost plans tend to have higher deductibles and higher annual out-of-pocket limits. But a person who can obtain medical services within a plan's network of providers often pays nothing for a visit to a primary care physician or the purchase of a generic drug. Treatments by a specialist typically incur a co-pay, while emergency room visits and out-patient surgeries come with capped costs that can vary from company to company.

It's important to note here that Advantage plan participants must still pay the Part B monthly premium.

Part D: Prescription drug coverage

Part D covers prescription drugs and offers coverage not included in Medicare Parts A and B. These coverage plans are offered by health insurance companies and come with a monthly premium that varies with

---

[16] Cate Deventer. Value Penquin. January 16, 2024. "What's the Cost of a Medicare Advantage Plan?" https://www.valuepenguin.com/medicare-advantage-plan-cost#

the level of coverage provided. Many plans are available in a range from $25 to $55.

Like Part B coverage, Part D participation is optional. But as is the case with Part B, Medicare will impose a 10 percent penalty on every monthly premium for every twelve-month period in which a late enrollee could have had Part D coverage but elected not to take it.

Under Part D coverage, drugs are grouped in tiers for pricing purposes. Most generic prescription drugs in the lower tiers are available for $0. Higher tier drugs, including many of the brand-name drugs advertised on TV, come with a higher cost, often a percentage of the full price.

Different plans offer different coverages, and we can help you find a plan with the most favorable coverage of the prescriptions in your medicine cabinet.

Medigap coverage

Most people of retirement age already know, long before we just reminded you, that Medicare Part B generally pays only 80 percent of non-hospital charges.

The 20 percent gap may not seem like much. That is until you consider the 20 percent share of, let's say, heart bypass surgery.

The average cost for such a life-saving procedure in the US is $123,000.[17] And while Medicare Part A will cover the costs of the operating room and your hospital stay, the 20 percent share of fees from the cardiologist, the surgical team, the anesthetist, the pre- and post-op visits, medications, the cardio rehab center, and other assorted costs can run to tens of thousands of dollars.

How would you pay such a bill? We would suggest, for the sake of preserving your retirement savings, that you absolutely need an insurance plan that pays for what Medicare doesn't.

---

[17] Statistica. 2022. "Average cost of a heart bypass in Colombia, Mexico, and the United States in 2021" https://www.statista.com/statistics/980006/latin-america-heart-bypass-cost/

Such is the purpose of individual Medicare supplemental insurance policies, also known as Medigap coverage. These plans sold by health insurance companies come in different price ranges with different levels of coverage and are identified by letters A through N. In 2024, plans G and N are generally considered to cover most, if not all, of the Medigap hole.

What might one expect to pay for such supplemental coverage? Well, a lot depends on your current health, and coverage rates also vary in different parts of the country. For Tom, a soon-to-be sixty-five-year-old man who doesn't smoke but has Type 2 diabetes, a Plan G supplement that will cover almost everything Medicare doesn't might cost around $148 per month in 2024. A Plan N with slightly different coverage might cost $111, according to plans we checked on behalf of our fictional couple.

The choice of Medigap plans can be confusing when facing an alphabet soup of choices. Fortunately, we at Russell Total Wealth and Wellness work closely with a licensed insurance professional who can help you make a choice that is right for you, depending on your current and projected medical needs.

Let's say, for instance, you know you are about to need a knee replacement, and you're waiting for Medicare eligibility before going on the table. Here is a case where you might opt for a higher premium supplemental that will cover all or most of an upcoming medical expense. You will have an option in following years to change your plan during open enrollment periods beginning each October. Or, if you think your medical needs can be held in reasonable check, you could also switch to an Advantage plan.

Which option is right for you? Let's examine their nuances and help you decide.

Medicare enrollment

One of the most common questions we deal with involves Medicare enrollment, a timing issue that often hinges on whether you are still working or covered by an employer's group health plan at the time your turn sixty-five.

The issue often comes down to the Part B premium payment we discussed earlier. Remember, a person covered by a group health plan (as well as a spouse also covered under the plan) need not take the Part B coverage as long as they have the alternative coverage.

For others, the issue is simpler. A person receiving Social Security benefits is automatically enrolled in parts A and B. Their red, white, and blue Medicare card, along with a "welcome" package, will be sent via mail a few months prior to their sixty-fifth birthday. Coverage begins on the first day of the month of that birthday, and Part B premium payments will be withheld beginning that month.

That's the easy part.

But a lot of people work beyond age sixty-five or decide to wait until full retirement age (sixty-six, sixty-seven, or some point in between) to begin receiving their full Social Security benefit. Some may choose to delay the start of Social Security to as late as age seventy to receive an enhanced benefit. What are their options?

Well, as indicated above, a Medicare-eligible person (and a spouse) who is covered by a group health plan – the "creditable coverage" concept – can decline Part B coverage, along with its monthly premium, until the group coverage ends. At that point they have eight months of a special enrollment period to sign up for coverage. Keep in mind that they are subject to a possible penalty should they fail to enroll in this time frame.

The Medicare website offers a tip for people described in the situation above. Because Part A benefits come without a premium to most people, Medicare suggests that those working past age sixty-five and still covered by group insurance to enroll in Medicare at the earliest opportunity. They will receive Part A coverage while being able to opt out of Part B. (We thought we'd pass that along.)

Things get a bit more complicated for a person not yet receiving Social Security and not covered by a group plan.

To avoid a penalty, such a person is advised to enroll in Medicare at the earliest opportunity. This is during an eight-month period that includes three months before their sixty-fifth birthday, the month of the birthday, and three months after. Failure to enroll during this period could delay enrollment to the next regular open enrollment period. We'll repeat this again because it can be a costly mistake: you can incur a 10 percent penalty on every monthly Part B premium you will ever pay for every twelve-month period in which you were eligible for Part B coverage and declined to take it.

One final note on Medicare enrollment.

Anyone not automatically enrolled – that is, anyone not yet receiving Social Security benefits – enrolls for Medicare through the Social Security Administration. You can do this online at www.ssa.gov/benefits/medicare, by calling the SSA at 1-800-772-1213, or by visiting a local or regional SSA office.

One other thing to remember if calling or making an in-person visit to a Social Security office: Patience is a virtue, and you may need all the virtue you can muster. Stay positive. Keep in mind that you'll be talking about money that will be paid to you for the rest of your life.

Funding long-term care (LTC)

The unpleasant prospect of needing and funding long-term nursing care is one of the most distressing issues awaiting people of retirement age. There are so many worries and so many questions, most of them negative in nature. What are the chances that either I or a spouse – or, God help us, both of us – will need long-term care? How can I avoid being a burden on my family? Can I afford an extended stay in a reasonably nice nursing facility? Will there be anything left for my heirs at the end?

Well, there are only two ways we know of to deal with the prospect of needing additional care in our advanced years. The first, not living until "old age," isn't one we even want to consider. The second, plan and prepare, we're ready to discuss.

Let's deal with the first question: What are my chances of needing long-term care?

Reports reveal that an American turning sixty-five has a 70 percent chance of needing some kind of long-term care in their remaining years.

The average stay in a long-term care facility is 3.2 years, but 20 percent of those admitted will require it for longer than five years.[18]

Now, the second question: Will I become a burden on my loved ones? This is a tougher question to answer because, frankly, it largely depends on the feelings of the people to whom you might turn to for care.

Some adults welcome their elderly parents into their homes, especially if Mom or Dad is still reasonably alert and able to provide in part for themselves. Others would prefer their parents to live elsewhere, something their folks might also desire when choosing whether to remain in the family home or consider moving to a senior living center.

Some adult children start out with the best of intentions – "We have a spare room that Mom can use, so why not have her live with us?" – but over time realize they can no longer give a parent with cognitive problems or special needs all the care they require. They turn to outside help, either through in-home services, assisted living, or extended nursing home care.

What kind of expenses might you be looking at if such outside care is needed?

In its report comparing long-term costs, Nationwide provides variations of estimated costs in each state.

Let's look at what the 2024 Nationwide report cited for Ohio, looking at figures for the state in general and the numbers for Dayton, Cincinnati and Columbus:

---

[18] Claire Samuels. a Place for Mom. September 13, 2023. "Long-Term Care Statistics: A Portrait of Americans in Assisted Living, Nursing Homes, and Skilled Nursing Facilities" https://www.aplaceformom.com/senior-living-data/articles/long-term-care-statistics

MEDIAN MONTHLY COSTS[19]

In-home services				
	Ohio	Dayton	Cincinnati	Columbus
Informal care	$3,112	$3,036	$3,448	$3,271
Home care	$3,130	$3,226	$3,092	$3,115
Community/assisted living				
	Ohio	Dayton	Cincinnati	Columbus
Assisted living facility	$5,386	$6,574	$5,901	$5,467
Nursing home care				
	Ohio	Dayton	Cincinnati	Columbus
Nursing home	$8,522	$9,228	$10,178	$8,459

The above figures, remember, are *monthly* estimates. Multiply those over a period of two or three years and it becomes easy to see how long-term care at any level can cut the legs from under even the best of retirement income plans. Finding alternative ways of paying for any of these expenses should be a significant part of any retirement plan.

And here is where we must break some bad news to some people. We're sorry to tell those who believe that Medicare will pay for sustained long-term nursing care that this simply *is not the case.* It would be nice to have such support, but it won't be coming from Medicare.

Perhaps people get confused upon learning that Medicare Part A will pay for a *limited stay* of twenty days in a skilled nursing facility following a qualifying in-patient hospital stay. But this does not apply to long-term custodial care needed for a patient who is not likely to recover from the condition that renders them unable to care for themselves.

Perhaps some confuse Medicare with *Medicaid.* This government health care program for people of lower incomes *will provide* coverage for long-term nursing care. Qualifying for Medicaid involves a complicated spending down of assets, and frankly, we prefer that our clients be in a position where they never need to even consider the Medicaid option.

---

[19] Nationwide. 2024. "Compare long-term care costs from state to state" https://nationwidefinancialltcmap.hvsfinancial.com/ 1

For years, a traditional approach to funding long-term care (LTC) involved purchasing traditional LTC insurance. But this may not always be the right option. Make sure you consider all options, especially given some other alternatives on today's insurance spectrum.

Traditional LTC insurance may, in fact, be the most comprehensive form of coverage. But it is also the most expensive way to go, and one of the most difficult to qualify for, in our opinion.

If you can get it cheaply – as some people can in their fifties when they are still relatively healthy and can still be underwritten for it – kudos to you. Regardless, premiums are likely to increase over time, likely potentially dramatically so. It's also possible that by the time you need this coverage, the premiums may be more than you can handle or some medical issue will disqualify you from coverage. Moreover, it's possible that you won't even need this coverage – we hope that's the case for you – and you will have nothing to show for years of paid premiums.

(There are LTC policies today that offer return of premium riders, an inducement to get people more interested, but we're still not completely sold.)

The life insurance option for LTC

Our coverage preference involves whole life insurance with an option that allows use of the death benefit when needed for long-term care. Some of today's annuity contracts also allow an accelerated benefit payment when needed for LTC.

Here's how it works.

Let's say you a whole life insurance policy with a $250,000 death benefit. A "living benefit" rider on the policy might allow use of up to half of the death benefit, $125,000, if needed for LTC. The rider would be triggered when the insured is unable to perform two of the six activities of daily living. (Activities of daily living are defined as the skills needed to manage one's basic physical needs. They include personal hygiene, grooming, dressing, toileting, eating, and transferring/ambulating.)

Now for example, let's also consider an annuity contract with an income value of $400,000. This contract has a 5 percent annual payout rate that produces $20,000 each year. If the annuitant requires LTC, and if their annuity allows it, the annual payout rate might be doubled and $40,000 becomes available for LTC funding for a period of time.

The annuity option is a consideration for people with medical conditions that prevent them from being underwritten for life insurance. No such underwriting is needed to own an annuity.

We should point out here that using these living benefits and accelerated payments will reduce the death benefit on the life insurance policy and the cash value of the annuity. This might be a viewed as a drawback for people who want a large death benefit available for heirs or who hope to pass on the remaining cash value of an annuity. But we like the idea of using the benefits of insurance products when you are still alive and need them. Coupled with the other benefits of life insurance – income protection via a tax-free death benefit for a surviving spouse or other beneficiaries – the hybrid approach of funding LTC through insurance products other than traditional long-term care insurance is something we look into to see if it makes sense for many of our clients.

Health Savings Accounts

Don't overlook the role of the Health Savings Account (HSA) as a tax-friendly health-care option in your pre-Medicare years. (HSA contributions cannot be made once Medicare begins, though tax-free withdrawals are allowed anytime if used for qualified medical expenses.)

Sadly, many people don't take advantage of the HSA option, in our opinion. IRS rules allow people with a "high deductible health plan," defined (in 2024) as plans with an annual deductible of $1,600 for individual coverage or $3,200 for family coverage or more, to make tax-deductible contributions to an account that can be used to pay out-of-pocket health care costs, including some co-pays, deductibles, and many charges associated with long-term nursing care.

Let's also note that while HSA accounts cannot be used to pay premiums for traditional health insurance and Medigap supplementals, they can be used to pay premiums on both long-term care policies and COBRA coverage. Moreover, HSA accounts can be used to pay for Medicare coverage for persons age sixty-five and older, an option that might be beneficial to Jeannie.[20] The amount that can be withdrawn tax-free is limited annually depending on one's age, and that allowable amount gets larger as one grows older.

Annual contributions are also limited. In 2024, an individual can contribute up to $4,150 and a couple up to $8,300.[21] Both an employee and an employer can contribute to the account. Employee contributions reduce taxable income in the year they are made and have the potential to grow through any investment option chosen by the account holder. Money withdrawn from the account is not taxed if used for qualified medical expenses.

In our view, the chance to grow a pool of potentially tax-free money for future health-care needs, to say nothing of the tax break realized when investing in the account, make the HSA a planning tool that can be used both before and after retirement.

It's now a bit after four. It's Bengals time. Jeannie joins Tom in the TV room, and their minds will be completely free of retirement thoughts for the next three-and-a-half hours. But let's sneak in one last thought before we lose them.

Don't forget to do frequent reviews of your retirement health care coverage, preferably with your advisor or an InsuranceMedicare Professional with whom they work closely. Here at Russell Total Wealth and Wellness, we routinely work with insurance professionals when we review a client's health insurance to help make sure it reflects any medical changes.

And now it's off to The Jungle.

---

[20] IRS. 2021. "Publication 969: Health Savings Accounts and Other Tax-Favored Health Plans." https://www.irs.gov/forms-pubs/about-publication-969

[21] Fidelity. May 10, 2024. "HSA contribution limits and eligibility rules for 2024 and 2025" https://www.fidelity.com/learning-center/smart-money/hsa-contribution-limits

CHAPTER 8

Sunday Night: The Road Ahead

It's now half past seven on a quiet Sunday evening. Tom and Jeannie are having a late, light dinner shortly after watching the Bengals run a perfect two-minute offense to set up a game-winning field goal with no time on the clock to beat the Ravens. They both feel good about that result.

They also feel good about the retirement research they've done over the course of the weekend, and they talk about some of what they've learned over dinner.

Whether they realize it or not, they now have the information they need – or at least know what they need to look for – to make their retirement decision.

This doesn't mean, mind you, that they'll make up their minds tonight or tomorrow or next week or next year. The purpose of this whole exercise, and the goal of this book, is to help you look at the things you need to consider before making a retirement decision, one you can make with confidence at the time of your choosing.

Tom, for example, has learned enough over the weekend to become comfortable with the idea of retiring in just a few months when he turns sixty-five.

He'll be eligible for Medicare then, which eliminates his biggest concern about having health insurance after leaving his employer's plan. He's still undecided about whether to apply for Social Security benefits. But he's got some time to think about his options: whether to start his benefits "early" and receive a slightly reduced benefit or to wait until his full benefit is available upon reaching full retirement age at sixty-six-and-ten-months. He's confident though, based on the research he and his wife just did, that they can produce the monthly income they need no matter which option he chooses.

Tom is ready for his "Johnny Paycheck moment" – an admittedly old-school reference to the country music artist who sang "Take This Job and Shove It." (Though we trust he'll submit his retirement notice with more class.)

Jeannie, however, isn't so sure.

She still has some issues of concern. Foremost among them is securing health insurance for herself once her coverage on Tom's plan ends with his retirement. She also worries about building up some means to pay the Medicare premiums she must eventually pay out-of-pocket as someone not eligible to receive Social Security.

She has a lot of questions. Her research throughout the weekend told her that she doesn't know all she needs to know before making her retirement decision. This, too, is a natural outgrowth of the weekend's planning.

It's time to get some help

Tom and Jeannie have learned a lot over the past three days, just as you've done in reading this deeply into this book. Thank you for staying with us and congratulations on the work you've done. Our hope at this point is you've gotten a more clearly defined view of the road that lies ahead, the journey into this potentially exciting time known as retirement.

And maybe, just maybe, you now realize you may need additional help in navigating this road.

You no doubt now appreciate that some retirement issues, especially those involving tax-saving strategies and estate planning, will require special help from CPAs and estate attorneys. Even dealing with routine questions –When should I turn on Social Security? Can I afford health insurance before Medicare kicks in? What are my Medigap options? –

can require the help of a Retirement Planner such as the members of our team at Russell Total Wealth and Wellness.

Let's be frank about something here.

Just as a skilled general practitioner isn't someone you want doing a cardiac procedure, it's also likely that your very competent Broker may notnecessarily be your best choice as a Retirement Planner, in our opinion.

Jeannie, remember, has an investment advisor, one she likes and who has done a nice job of helping her establish and grow her 403(b). But now Jeannie faces retirement-specific concerns about health care coverage, Medicare costs and survivor issues. She feels a bit overwhelmed by all she has learned this weekend – things she's never discussed with her accumulation advisor. She wonders if her investment advisor – a good source of information on mutual funds and ETFs – isn't a bit overmatched when it comes to dealing with, say, Medicare supplemental insurance costs and options.

Jeannie, like many readers of this book, has more questions than she thought she would. Fortunately, we can help answer your questions that may be similar to what we discussed.

We'll highlight more specifically what to look for in a retirement-specific advisor in our wrap-up Chapter Ten. For now, let's discuss what you've done for yourself at the end of our three-day retirement-consideration period.

We hope you feel good about what you've learned about yourself and where you stand on the verge of retirement. For many people, this review is really the first time they've taken a deep-dive look into what they've invested and saved, how much they might expect to spend in retirement, or what kind of income will they have when they no longer receive a regular paycheck from employment.

Our goal is to help our clients feel more confident about their retirement once they go through this process. We hope that this will give them an idea of where they are at in their journey to retirement and what they need to start for their next steps.

But we also have a word of caution, one any coach would give to a team sitting on a big lead going into the fourth quarter.

The game isn't over yet. Retirement may be a goal, but it isn't the finish line. You've still got some playing time left, and you need to handle it responsibly. You've played the game well to this point. Let's not drop the ball now.

When the outlook isn't so bright

We're sad to report not everyone will see this pretty picture.

After a weekend of both review and looking ahead, some will find their retirement savings are not what they need to be. Their mindset could, and should, be changed. They realize, sometimes for the first time, that they may have to work longer than they planned. They will have to save more. They will probably have to spend less.

Their retirement dream may not be all that they envisioned. Not yet, anyway. But that doesn't mean the view today must necessarily be the one you will see forever.

There are always adjustments to be made, even relatively later in life. As noted above, maybe you'll work longer than you'd planned or take on part-time employment during retirement. Perhaps you need to top out your contributions to your company's 401(k) or, preferably, to your personal Roth IRA. Maybe you'll delay starting Social Security until your benefit is maximized at age seventy. Maybe you'll scale down your long-terms retirement dreams a bit and change your plans for a dream trip to Napoli to an extended stay in the Napa Valley or Naples, Florida.

We are here to help you make these "catchup" adjustments.

The sixty-two-year-old Jeannie, for example, now knows she faces such adjustments. She realizes she could address several concerns – finding health insurance after Tom's retirement and funding future Medicare premiums – by continuing to work. But that's easier said than done.

Like so many teachers in 2020, she was worn down by the stress of having to teach remotely when schools were closed during the Covid pandemic. She struggles to put the horrifying prospect of school shootings in the back of her mind, but the thought is never far away. And while she will always love her students, the demands and restraints put on teachers from parents and school boards alike are becoming increasingly troublesome, more so than at any other time in her career.

She wonders how long she can resist the urge to follow so many of her fellow teachers out of the profession.

When we have clients come in we would look to see what options they may have available for health insurance coverage. Depending on where they work, they may be eligible for certain programs through the state, or they may be eligible for COBRA coverage. They can also consider a private group health coverage plan offered by a Dayton company that we are familiar with. In addition, we always try to encourage clients to build a pool of funds to account for future Medicare premiums they will have to pay out-of-pocket.

Jeannie knows both she and Tom will have to pay $174.40 a month (as of 2024) in Part B premiums. She also will likely have to pay her Part A premium of at least $278 as a non-recipient of Social Security. To help plan for this expense, one option she could consider would be to change her 403(b) contributions into those for a Roth IRA from which she can take future tax-free distributions to pay for Medicare premiums or Medigap supplemental insurance.

Another option, she may consider is to contribute to a Health Savings Account in which her current contributions are tax deductible but future distributions are tax free when used for qualifying medical expenses, including paying Medicare premiums and, if needed, long-term care expenses.

Should Jeannie feel the need to retire sooner than later, she and Tom will likely have to adjust their long-term income plan.

In our income planning chapter, we described how this couple – with both spouses retired – planned to draw $8,000 in monthly income to meet both recurring and "expected unexpected" expenses and another $2,000 monthly for the "bucket list" of fun things they hoped to do in retirement. If she retires before age sixty-five, Jeannie will likely have to pay health insurance premiums out of that "frill" part of the budget. And even after reaching Medicare age, she is looking at $450-plus in monthly out-of-pocket Medicare premiums that will likely force a change in their budgeting.

Again, it's better to know about and prepare for these budget-affecting possibilities now than when they hit you unexpectedly in retirement.

This, we would suggest, is the reason you need to spend a concentrated period of time – such as that outlined over our three-day weekend – to consider the important elements of retirement planning, things you haven't fully explored previously. This, we would also suggest, is where you need to work with a wealth advisor to help you with the things you can't easily do for yourself.

CHAPTER 9

Frequently Asked Questions, and Some Answers

We know we've thrown a lot of information at you over the previous eight chapters, and we thank you for sticking with us. We also know we didn't address everything, and you no doubt have questions at this point. We deal with many of them on an almost daily basis as we visit with new clients and help address the concerns of existing ones.

Even so, there are some questions we hear more often than others. We thought we might use this Frequently Asked Questions format to deal with some of the most common inquiries we get from people nearing or already into retirement.

Social Security earnings limits, "break-even" points, long-term viability

I'm getting conflicting information about working while receiving Social Security. Some friends say I can work and earn without limits. Others say I might lose some of my benefits when doing so. What's the story here?

There is truth in both statements, but neither tell the whole story.

Yes, a person who has reached their full retirement age (FRA) can work and earn as much as they can without having an impact on their monthly Social Security benefit. (Reminder: We have a chart showing FRA for people born in various years in our Chapter Three discussion of "mailbox income.")

However, things are a bit different for people who work while receiving Social Security before reaching FRA. The Social Security Administration imposes an "earnings test" on such people, and any wages earned above an annual limit (which typically increases each year) will result in a reduction of benefits. The SSA's reasoning for doing so is that people on Social Security who continue to receive wages at higher levels before reaching FRA aren't truly "retired."

In 2024, benefit recipients who've yet to reach FRA could earn up to $22,320 in total wages without a reduction in benefits. This earnings limit changes considerably – to $59,520 – for wages earned in the months of the calendar year in which you reach FRA. Upon reaching FRA, there is no earnings limit.

The SSA, upon learning of limit-exceeding earnings from either your tax return or your own self-reporting, will deduct $1 in future benefit payments for every $2 earned over the limit. For example, a person receiving Social Security before reaching FRA who earns $29,080 in 2024 has earned $6,760 over the limit. The SSA will deduct half of that, $3,380, from future benefit checks until the "takeback" is realized.

Things get a bit more generous for over-the-limit wages earned in the months of the year in which you reach FRA. Not only does the earnings limit go up, but the "takeback" is reduced to $1 deducted for every $3 over the limit.[22]

But don't be discouraged from working. The money taken back through reduced benefits is not "lost." Upon reaching FRA, the SSA will return the money it withheld in the form of increased benefits until the "takeback" amount is fully returned.

So, if you choose to work while taking Social Security benefits "early," do so advisedly. Your benefits might be reduced on a short-term basis, even though this reduction will be returned to you eventually.

---

[22] Andy Markowitz. AARP. December 7, 2023. "When does the earnings limit on Social Security benefits expire?" When Does The Earnings Limit End for Social Security? (aarp.org)

I've heard financial advisors on radio programs – and I think one of them might have been your show on WHIO – talk about "break even" points in Social Security benefits. What is this all about?

"Break-even" generally refers to a point in time at which the total amount of Social Security benefits received become equal whether they are first taken "early" (beginning as early as age sixty-two), or at FRA (either at age sixty-six, sixty-seven, or sometime in between), or even later when delayed retirement credits increase a monthly benefit by 8 percent for each twelve-month period between FRA and age seventy.

You likely know that the amount of your monthly benefit is affected by when you first take it. (You know this, in part, because you read it in our third chapter.) Let's do a brief review anyway.

You will receive your full work-history benefit at FRA. But if you begin taking benefits prior to FRA, each monthly payment will be permanently reduced by a fixed percentage for each month between your starting point and your FRA. The Social Security Administration imposes a reduction of five-ninths of 1 percent for each month a benefit is collected before FRA, up to thirty-six months. For each additional month past that three-year period, the reduction is five-twelves of 1 percent.[23] (Example: A person with an FRA of sixty-seven who begins receiving benefits at age sixty-two will see their monthly check reduced by 30 percent, according to the SSA.) Conversely, a person at FRA sixty-seven who delays benefits until age seventy might see their monthly check increased by as much as 24 percent (three years times an 8 percent increase each year.)

Now, let's explore "break even points" by doing some math with the help of the authoritative AARP.

Using its Social Security calculator, the AARP projects that a person born in 1960 (FRA, sixty-seven) who averaged $50,000 over their top thirty-five earning years would receive a benefit of $1,927 monthly if first taking benefits at FRA. That benefit would be reduced to $1,349 (a

---

[23] Andy Markowitz. AARP. December 13, 2023. "How much does early retirement reduce Social Security benefits?" How Does Early Retirement Affect Social Security? (aarp.org)

30 percent decrease) if started at age sixty-two but increased to $2,389 (a 24 percent increase) if delayed until age seventy.[24]

The person above who starts Social Security "early" will receive more payments, but at a reduced amount, than a person starting at FRA or later. A person starting benefits at age 70 will receive fewer payments than the early or FRA starter, but each payment will be larger.

Using the above figures, let's look at how the total amount of benefits received by the three people just described compare at different ages.

At age 78		
Starting age/ monthly benefit*	Payments received	Total benefits
62/$1,349	192	$259,008
67/$1,927	132	$254,364
70/$2,389	96	$229,344
At age 80		
Starting age/ monthly benefit*	Payments received	Total benefits
62/$1,349	216	$291,384
67/$1,927	156	$300,612
70/$2,389	120	$286,680
At age 82		
Starting age/ monthly benefit*	Payments received	Total benefits
62/$1,349	240	$323,760
67/$1,927	180	$346,860
70/$2,389	144	$344,016
At age 83		
Starting age/ monthly benefit*	Payments received	Total benefits
62/$1,349	252	$339,945
67/$1,927	192	$369,984
70/$2,389	156	$372,684

* Does not account for cost-of-living increases

---

[24] AARP. May 25, 2022. "Social Security Calculator." https://www.aarp.org/retirement/social-security/benefits-calculator

The numbers tell the story. At age seventy-eight, the person beginning Social Security at age sixty-two has a slight advantage in total benefits over their two peers. Two years later, however, the person starting at FRA has the edge. By age eighty-two, the FRA and age seventy starters are almost equal, but a year after that, a "seventy starter" has an edge that will only continue to grow as time allows.

As we said earlier in the book, your decision on when to begin taking Social Security depends on many factors, some known only to you. Longevity is a big factor, and people who delay taking benefits and are fortunate to live into their eighties and beyond will most likely end up with a larger package of Social Security benefits. On the other hand, people who delay taking benefits and pass before reaching a normal American life expectancy could end up leaving money on the table when compared to those who've been receiving smaller benefits for longer periods of time.

It goes without saying that none of us know how long we might live. But a discussion with a financial professional – a talk that will discuss your current health, your family history of longevity, and your current financial situation – will help you better understand your Social Security options.

While we're on the subject of Social Security, what are your views on the long-term viability of the program? I'm approaching the age where I can make my Social Security decision at any time of my choosing, but I'm worried about my adult children now in their forties. Will Social Security be there when their time comes to collect? And a follow-up: What kind of changes might you envision coming in their future?

From Andie Doller: I believe Social Security will be there for people who are currently in their forties, but I also believe it will likely look different than the current plan does today. I anticipate another change to the full retirement age, potentially moving from age sixty-seven to seventy. I also think a change to the "early retirement age" may be in line. If they make these changes sooner rather than later, it will feel like a minimal change to those who are still fifteen to twenty-five years away from retirement, just as it did the last time the FRA was adjusted up from sixty-five.

That said, as someone in their forties, I'm not banking on Social Security to be a big part of my retirement income strategy. By that I mean that while I believe there will be money forthcoming, I'm not counting on receiving the amount Social Security says is due me. Sure, I can check my account today on SocialSecurity.gov and it might tell me I will get, say, $3,000 a month at my FRA. Well, I need a little more certainty than that, especially given the changes I anticipate are coming, before I start calculating that estimate into my retirement income plan.

I'd suggest that others in their forties consider following the same thought process. That is, ***something*** will be coming our way from Social Security, but it's too early to tell exactly how much that may be. My suggestion is that we should plan on funding our retirement in a way in which Social Security is more like icing on the cake rather than the biggest part of the meal.

From Curvin Miller: I concur with what Andie has written and would add that we are likely to see a reduction in future benefits from a program that is projected to be less than 100 percent fully funded by the mid-2030s. Given how U.S. programs have operated in the past, In my opinion, I wouldn't be surprised to see the Social Security Administration pay a reduced benefit to people born after a specified year, say, 1990 or later.

I also would not be surprised to see an increase in the Social Security and Medicare taxes that are routinely withheld from our regular paychecks.

Medicare premium surcharges, and who is IRMAA?

Please explain how it is that people earning over a certain annual amount may face paying higher Medicare Part B premiums?

Meet IRMAA, who is not, as the name might suggest, an especially nice lady to roughly 7 percent of people who pay Medicare Part B premiums.

IRMAA stands for Income Related Monthly Adjustment Amounts. Translated, this is Medicare's way of imposing a surcharge on Part B premiums paid by some of America's higher earners. IRMAA is based on the Modified Adjustment Gross Income (MAGI) reported on your annual tax return. Single filers with a MAGI exceeding $103,000, and married filers with more than $206,000 will pay higher monthly Part B premiums.

Most Americans in 2024 paid $174.40 monthly for Part B coverage. The first level of the IRMAA surcharge raised that premium to $244.30, and there are four additional step-ups beyond that as reflected in the chart below.[25]

---

[25] IRMAA Certified Planner. 2024. "Official IRMAA 2024 Brackets" https://www.irmaacertifiedplanner.com/2024-irmaa-brackets/

Full Part B Coverage

Beneficiaries who file individual tax returns with modified adjusted gross income:	Beneficiaries who file joint tax returns with modified adjusted gross income:	Income-Related Monthly Adjustment Amount	Total Monthly Premium Amount
Less than or equal to $103,000	Less than or equal to $206,000	$0.00	$174.70
Greater than $103,000 and less than or equal to $129,000	Greater than $206,000 and less than or equal to $258,000	$69.90	$244.60
Greater than $129,000 and less than or equal to $161,000	Greater than $258,000 and less than or equal to $322,000	$174.70	$349.40
Greater than $161,000 and less than or equal to $193,000	Greater than $322,000 and less than or equal to $386,000	$279.50	$454.20
Greater than $193,000 and less than $500,000	Greater than $386,000 and less than $750,000	$384.30	$559.00
Greater than or equal to $500,000	Greater than or equal to $750,000	$419.30	$594.00

[26]

This income-related surcharge, which began in 2007, affects about 7 percent of Medicare recipients. If you happen to be among this unlucky few, you might consider building up your tax-free resources as a source of future income in retirement as money taken from tax-free accounts (such as the Roth IRA or Roth 401(k)) does not count as part of your MAGI number.

---

[26] Ibid.

The role of the independent advisor

I heard you talking at a dinner about how your firm was an "independent" company as opposed to a "captive" one. What's the difference?

The term "captive advisor" is often used in our industry to describe agents or advisors employed by the kind of large national financial services firms you are likely to see advertised on network primetime shows and major sports events. Such individuals can be very capable people who sell appropriate investment products, but they also can be limited to offering only the products offered by their parent company.

As an independent company, we are not married to a larger parent firm telling us what we ***must use*** when offering services to our clients. As independents, we are able to offer a wide range of products and services to help better serve our clients.

I'm an Ohio public employee and will soon – I hope – receive a state-funded pension. My friends who retired before me tell me I need to carefully consider what kind of "payout options" I want to receive. What kind of options are they talking about?

A person fortunate enough to receive a pension these days – and congratulations to our questioner for being one – has any number of options to consider in how they will receive their regular pension payments. Among the most common options:

- Life guaranteed. Pension payments are guaranteed for the life of the pensioner, but the payments stop at the time of the worker's death.
- Life with spouse guaranteed which assures payments over the life of both the worker and a surviving spouse. Payments under this provision are generally lower than those made in a single-life guarantee.
- A time-period guarantee. Payments are guaranteed to be made to someone – either the worker, a spouse, or designated beneficiary(s) – over a specified period, be it anywhere from five to twenty or more years. The payments cease at the end of the designated period. A shorter guaranteed period creates a larger regular payout.

There are other "mix-and-match" options to consider, and your individual income needs will affect the option you choose. A pensioner might, for example, choose a life-with-survivor at 75 or 50 percent option. This pays the full benefit over the life of the worker, but only a reduced benefit to a surviving spouse. The worker essentially sets up a pay cut for the survivor in exchange for a higher payment for themselves over the course of their lifetime.

My brother-in-law recently incurred a penalty for failing to take his proper required minimum distribution (RMD) for the year. Admittedly, he's not above trying to stay one step ahead of the IRS. But in this case, he claims he wasn't told of a tax qualified amount from the financial firm holding his 401(k). Assuming he's telling the truth – and that might be a reach – wasn't it the company's responsibility to notify him?

It is true that financial services firms who hold your tax-deferred money – be it in an IRA, 401(k), 403(b), or other qualified retirement account – routinely notify you of your account balance as of the end of each year. Persons required to make RMDs beginning at age seventy-three must do so based on the total of all their qualified funds at the end of the previous year.

However, the bottom line is that anyone facing an RMD is obligated to make their own correct determination of the amount to be withdrawn. The old "I never got a notice" excuse just won't fly here. A person with tax-deferred money is required to know how much they have. And while the financial custodians holding these funds are routinely helpful, it's sometimes possible to lose track of where all your money is, particularly when it's spread among several different firms.

This has probably happened only a handful of times over our two careers, but we've encountered people who've truly forgotten about qualified money that has yet to be taxed. One example that crossed our desk involved a man who had a 401(k) plan with a company he left many years ago. This individual had moved since finding a new job, but his former employer had no knowledge of the new address. The custodian company would send out the required notices only to find them returned as undeliverable.

HOW TO RETIRE IN A WEEKEND | 97

Here's something else to consider. The failure to take a correct RMD might not get detected in the first year, maybe even the first two. Keep in mind that Form 5498 – which reports the amount in your qualified accounts – goes to the IRS just as it goes to you, the IRA owner. Uncle Sam will find out about these funds eventually, and when he does, his penalty is 25 percent on any amount you should have withdrawn but didn't(This penalty could be reduced to 10 percent if it is caught and corrected promptly).[27] You want to make sure you are taking the right amount of RMD each year when obligated to do so.

This is another argument for reducing your pool of tax-deferred money ahead of the time when you must begin withdrawing it and paying tax as you do so. Doing Roth IRA conversions in the years before RMD age gives you more control over when you withdraw your qualified money as well as the opportunity to experience future tax-free growth and tax-free distributions from Roth accounts at a time of your choosing.

All this talk about the difference between an "accumulation" advisor and a "distribution" advisor is a bit confusing. My current advisor says there is no reason she can't serve both functions. Is she right?

Maybe she can and maybe she can't. Still, our experience tells us that different professionals offer different specialties for different times of life. The best general practitioner in your clinic, for instance, isn't necessarily someone you'd want to see for a cancer treatment or a hip replacement. Along those same lines, Mt. Everest climbing expeditions often utilize one sherpa – the Tibetan natives who serve as guides – on the ascent phase and a different one for the descent. This is likely because, statistically, more fatalities occur on the trip down the mountain after climbers are exhausted by the trip up.

The road to retirement is your trip up Everest in this analogy. But the "accumulation advisor" who may have done a fine job in helping grow

---

[27] IRS. December 20, 2023. "IRS reminds those aged 73 and older to make required withdrawals from IRAs and retirement plans by Dec. 31; notes changes in the law for 2023" https://www.irs.gov/newsroom/irs-reminds-those-aged-73-and-older-to-make-required-withdrawals-from-iras-and-retirement-plans-by-dec-31-notes-changes-in-the-law-for-2023

your assets and getting to a goal – that is, the allegorical mountain summit – may not be as skilled in the distribution/descent phase of retirement. Your trip back down the mountain is a time when taking income from your lifetime of savings – and making that money last as long as you do – becomes your dominant concern. You can't afford to stumble and fall on this important phase of your life's expedition.

Look, we're not saying that the person who helped you get **to retirement** can't help you get **through retirement**. But just as there are specialists in medicine, law, and even mountain climbing, so too are there Advisors in retirement living. At Russell, we take pride in assisting retirement-age people in both the distribution and preservation of their life savings. That's not to say, mind you, that we can't help younger clients in their accumulation phase of life; we do that as well. We often work with the children of long-established clients, sometimes after they inherit from parents who've been with us for years. But our emphasis and focus is retirement planning and income generation throughout the period that should be one of the most enjoyable parts of your life's journey.

The inner workings of annuities

Here's something I've never completely understood about annuities. I keep hearing about how they can provide income for life, but I've also heard that the annuity value decreases as payments are made. My question: Can an annuity "run out of money," and if so, what happens then?

Good question, and the short but incomplete answer is: It depends on how the annuity is structured and the payment options established when the contract was written.

An annuity that does not have an income rider or is not annuitized – and we'll explain both concepts here shortly – has the potential for the account value to fall to $0 if all the money invested and grown in the contract is paid out over time. Payments would cease for such a contract.

However, an "income rider" – an option that can be added to an annuity contract (usually, but not always, at an additional cost) – can be structured to contractually obligate the insurance company to continue making payments even if the contract value falls to $0, which can happen as payments erode the contract value. The rider is basically insurance against the contract running out of money and failing to generate income. This promise to make payments is guaranteed by the claims-paying ability of the insurance company issuing the annuity contract.

A word of caution here. There are typically a lot of rules and nuances involved with income riders, and they are not all created equal. It is important to understand how your specific income rider works.

A contract that is "annuitized" also requires the insurance company to make payments to the annuitant over the period of time designated in the contract. As is the case with pension payments described above, the contracted period might cover the lifetime of the annuitant, or the annuitant and a surviving spouse. Payments might also be guaranteed to someone – either the annuitant or a beneficiary(s) – for a time-certain period of, say, ten or twenty years. Payments are calculated to last over the designated amount of time.

But annuitization is a rather "old-school" concept that is rarely used in annuities issued in the past decade or so. There was a time when annuitants seeking guaranteed lifetime income would annuitize a contract, a process that put an obligation on the insurer but also gave full control of the contract to the insurance company unless the annuity offers an enhanced death benefit feature, which usually involves an additional cost. In an annuitized contract, any money remaining in the account after the death of the annuitant goes to the insurance company. In a non-annuitized contract, any money remaining after payouts can go to a designated beneficiary(s).

The development of income riders negated the need for annuitization – a good development, in our opinion – though the option remains available (if rarely used) today.

I've heard you discuss how an annuity can be used to pay for long-term nursing care. I have two annuities, but neither– as best as I can see – allow for this possibility. What are my options if I want to add a long-term care provision to any of these contracts?

Unfortunately, these options must be elected when the annuity policy is issued and cannot be added after the fact. If your current annuity contract does not allow for long-term care and if funding this care is a concern, it may be time to take a look and decide whether your current annuity is still a good fit and perhaps pursue one with newer features.

I'm a soon-to-retire investor, and I've become what many people would call "fairly conservative" in my investment approach over recent years. But I never completely left "the game," and consequently took some significant hits during the market downturn of 2022. I'm to the point that I can no longer accept these losses like I did in 2002 and 2008. What are my options if I want to "get out of the market" and still get some kind of return that at least keeps pace with inflation?

It's not uncommon for people, especially early in retirement, to want to get out of the market completely and eliminate what they see as risk. The challenge in doing so is that by avoiding one risk, you often pick up an entirely different set of risks. Here's what we mean by that.

In a low-interest rate environment, even if you were to take all your money out of the market and put it into a fixed-rate account, you're looking at a guaranteed loss each year. Why is that? Well, in mid-2022, the highest rate on any fixed-rate investment was about 4.25 percent. Yet year-over-year inflation in June of 2022 was 9.1 percent, the highest monthly hike in forty years. That's an almost 5 percent loss of purchasing power to inflation right there.

Fortunately, in 2024, higher interest rates became the norm and the inflation rate lowered, leading to greater opportunities for investors.

However, it's just impossible to avoid every kind of risk. We take some degree of risk every time we board a plane, drive our cars, or cross a busy street. There are, however, ways to reduce the risk we take in life. We buckle seat belts, eat more healthy foods, exercise more frequently, cross with the stop light, or stop smoking (or better yet, never start).

As we approach or enter retirement, we also look at ways to help mitigate the risk we take attempting to grow money in a way that will meet our future needs or outpace inflation. And here we'll respectfully suggest, yet again, that our trademarked, Fiscal House™ management philosophy is one such way that can help.

To recap, our Fiscal House™ is built on a foundation of money you can't afford to lose. This is money you want to preserve, but you also hope for at least some growth as a protection against future inflation.

This foundation will likely include money market accounts, CDs, fixed or indexed annuities, and/or multi-year guaranteed annuities. Again, this is money you cannot afford to do unless you choose to do so, such as in cashing out a CD early and incurring a penalty.

The walls of our Fiscal House™ are designed to help produce income with limited, non-correlated exposure to the market. We described several such income-producing or dividend-paying options in more detail back in Chapter Four.

Our house is then topped out by a roof of investments that are exposed to market risk (at whatever risk level you are comfortable assuming) in the hope of realizing continued growth. Any investments made here will be with money that *is not needed* for everyday expenses, or money you know you will not need soon.

Some people will put more into their roof than others. Some will want to stay in "the game," one they've perhaps played over much of their life and are comfortable with. Others, like our questioner here, will have only limited tolerance for the routine ups and downs of the market, and absolutely no stomach for the volatility of 2022.

So, responding to the original question, let's just say that an anxious retiree doesn't have to be either all-in or completely out of the market. There is middle ground between the two extremes and working with a financial professional – such as us – can help you find the right place for your unique situation.

What can I believe in all these TV ads?

I liked Tom Sellick in *Magnum PI*, and his commercials for reverse mortgages make a lot of sense to me. What do I need to know that maybe Magnum isn't telling me?

Reverse mortgages are the province of lending institutions, and we are not a lender and consequently don't deal with them. But from a purely commentary viewpoint, let's say this.

Be very, very careful when considering a reverse mortgage as an alternative source of retirement income. They are not right for everyone, yet they are advertised (using a popular compensated spokesman such as Sellick) to reach as broad an audience as possible.

In our view, you will more often than not get less value from a reverse mortgage than by selling your home outright. Remember, the lending company makes its money on the spread between what your house is worth – when they eventually sell it – and what they paid you for it. Yes, you can continue to live in your home under this arrangement, but we would suggest that if you do need immediate income for some need, a home equity loan that allows you to retain ownership might be a better option than a reverse mortgage.

We believe there are better ways to produce retirement income than taking what is essentially a loan against the future sale of your home. If you have other assets you can use for income – and our goal is to help you grow such assets – a reverse mortgage may not be right for you.

Speaking of ads, I'm waking up earlier as I get older and sometimes turn on the TV for background noise at 5:30 a.m. You can't believe (or maybe you can) the number of ads they show then for no-premium Medicare Advantage programs. How easy would it be to switch from my Medicare supplemental coverage (Medigap) to an Advantage plan? And, can I switch back at a later time?

It's relatively easy to switch from a Medicare supplemental plan to a lower-premium Advantage plan.

The difficulty, however, comes if you want to switch back to your previous (or any other) Medigap plan. Let's say you're facing a major upcoming medical need that you think might be better covered by your Medigap plan than your Advantage one. You can switch back relatively easily if done in the first twelve months of your initial enrollment in the Advantage plan. But if you switch back later than that, you must pass the insurance carrier's underwriting criteria in order to be accepted for coverage. The insurer will ask a series of questions about your current health, and any indication of major disease – coronary problems, stroke, cancer, kidney disease, etc. – could result in a denial of coverage.

I've heard that the RMD age may be going up in the future. Any chance of this happening?

Maybe a good chance, emphasis on the "maybe."

SECURE Act 2.0 further expanded some of the retirement-savings rule changes made by the original SECURE Act of 2019. That measure, among other things, moved the starting age for RMDs back from 70 1/2 to 72 for people who reached the later age in 2020 or later.

SECURE Act 2.0, which was passed in the final days of 2022 moved the RMD starting age back to seventy-three for those born between 1951 and 1959. For folks born after January 1, 1960, the RMD age moved to age seventy-five.[28]

Many members of Congress will tell you that the purpose of reforms like these are to get more Americans saving and investing for their retirement. Other more skeptical people will point out that any future delay of RMD age merely creates a bigger pool of tax-deferred money that Uncle Sam will eventually tap.

While we don't entirely disagree with the skeptics, we prefer to view this proposed new RMD age as an opportunity. If the seventy-five RMD starting age comes to pass, many Americans will have additional time to further drain their pool of tax-deferred money that will soon be taxed.

We repeat again our previous point urging people to make Roth IRA conversions when the most tax-advantageous time presents itself. We'd further suggest that such a time is available right now, or at any time before the tax cuts implemented in 2018 are scheduled to expire at the start of 2026.

One last question, this one for Curv: How do your Jackets look this season? And how 'bout them Bengals?

I'm always hopeful, but I don't expect the boys in Columbus to be kissing the Stanley Cup this season. But Burrow and the Bengals? I don't think their 2021 trip to the Super Bowl will be their last.

---

[28] National Society of Tax Professionals. May 30, 2023. "Secure Act 2.0 — When Does The RMD Start?" https://www.nstp.org/article/secure-act-2-0-%E2%80%93-when-does-the-rmd-start

CHAPTER 10

Choosing Your Guide on the Road Through Retirement

The end of our book brings us back to where we began, with a reminder it's, "it's five o-clock somewhere."

This phrase most likely refers to the start of cocktail hour at the end of a tough day, or perhaps a long weekend that begins with some much-needed TGIF time. But message could just as well be about retirement. After all, they're both at that age when you finally decide that you've reached the point in life when it's time to "just tell 'em I sailed away."

Perhaps by the time you've reached this concluding chapter, you will have learned enough to become comfortable with your own eventual retirement decision. No, this isn't necessarily an announcement you will make tomorrow, but it's one you can be comfortable with whenever you decide to "call it a day."

It's also likely that you still have questions and need further guidance. Our fictional couple in this book, Tom and Jeannie, pulled together a ton of essential retirement-age information over the course of the weekend. They did that on their own, just as you now can. A tip of the hat to all of you who now have at least a better view of where you stand, here on the verge of retirement, than you did before you began our three-day consideration process.

But their research, as well as yours, also showed them things they could not address on their own, issues that likely will require some professional guidance.

We are here to help. We are Retirement Planners who've spent a few decades helping people generate consistent income that will enable them to enjoy their years away from the daily workforce – however many years that might be. We're anxious to help develop a trusting, professional relationship in which we can serve as your guide along this road through retirement, a highway you've yet to travel and don't know as well as you would like.

Let's look at how we'll begin this journey together.

How to pick a retirement planner (and why you should consider us)

This idea of putting your financial affairs in the hands of someone you've never met before – or met only at an informational seminar/dinner, or heard or the radio, or learned about from reading this book – can sometimes be a high-anxiety decision for people. This is especially true for those who've never worked with an advisor or people who've had a bad experience with a previous one.

(Sidebar: If you've had a bad experience in the past, it's important to be honest with us and tell us what that experience was like. We don't want you to experience the same frustration twice.)

The process of building any relationship begins with establishing levels of both comfort and trust. At Russell Total Wealth and Wellness, we start this process – if we're blessed enough to have you schedule a visit to our office – with our proprietary On-Track Retirement Review. This is part of a ninety-minute introductory meeting we've developed and refined over a four-decade period that allows us to listen and better understand a new client's concerns, needs, goals, and (sometimes) fears.

Please note that this first meeting *is not* necessarily about changing what you're doing now or changing your current advisor (if you have one). Rather, it's more about finding out *what* you're doing now. This is your chance to sit down with a Wealth Advisor, someone you can talk to about the things that are most important to you. It's also our first chance to see if you are on the right path to getting where you want to be, something we need to know before even considering other options (if necessary) that might help you get there.

We need to know whether your current plan (if you have one) addresses all your questions and solves all concerns you might have. Tom and Jeannie, for example, answered a lot of their own questions, but also raised several others – ones we hear routinely from first-time visitors. Questions about when is the best time, in our specific situation, to begin taking Social Security? What are our Medicare and Medigap choices? What kind of pension-payout options are available, and what might work best for us? How might we adjust our income to handle future inflation? How can we keep our taxes reasonably low and pass on our assets to loved ones without undue taxes and hassles? And, most important, how do we make our money last for as long as we will need it?

Something we often find during a first visit with a prospective new client(s) is that their current "plan" is little more than a collection of different retirement investments. There is nothing that explains how all these investments will produce future income, or how much. And more importantly, how this income will survive for as long as the investors do. Their "plan," in essence, is really no plan at all.

Our On-Track Retirement Review is designed to help not only show us where you are today, but also to show you where you might be exposed to potential problems tomorrow. It includes a retirement "what-if" analysis that looks at any potential cracks and weaknesses in your plan, things that haven't happened yet but might in the future. These are things you need to pay attention to that might not have caught your attention yet.

Our ultimate objective is to help make sure you have a true action plan – a detailed, written blueprint, that projects how income will be provided to meet both your essential and discretionary needs over thirty or more years of retirement. This will be a plan that helps set a course for your financial future and no longer leaves you merely hoping that you can meet the goals you've set for yourself.

Let's also note here that establishing this relationship is a two-way street. Our goal is that a new client develops comfort and trust in us, which is both a "gut" and intellectual feeling. But we must also note that we don't take on everyone we visit as a client.

We must believe that a perspective client is as willing to work with us as we are to work with them. We need to believe that they can accept our honest and objective analysis about what they've accomplished so far, then listen to our advice on what they've yet to do. We may or may not be the right fit for everyone we encounter. But even if our philosophies don't align for a long-term business relationship, we believe we can still help provide a great deal of value in any meeting we have with prospective clients, or at least give them direction on what they need to consider.

Other areas of consideration

There are other questions you should ask of any financial services firm you might consider.

A firm's fee structure is at the top of the list for many people.

Three types of fee structures are common in most firms: A flat fee, billable hours, and fees for actively managed accounts. Our company doesn't charge a flat fee as we don't believe in a "cookie cutter" approach in which a plan can simply be pulled off the shelf and used for every client. Instead, we build plans that are tailored to each client's individual need. As an independent firm, when we provide investment advisory services we do charge a fee, but these fees will be discussed upon meeting.

You might also consider referrals when making your choice of an advisor.

As you are looking to determine which advisor you are comfortable meeting with, you should always do your research and check out any reviews left on them online. In addition, you can ask the advisor if they have any references.

Trust is an earned thing, and we believe that our On-Track Retirement Review gives both sides, client and advisor alike, the best chance to establish a long-term relationship.

We spend most of this first meeting learning about you. We listen to your story and get a better understanding about what's important to you. We get a feel for what you've done to prepare for retirement and an idea of some things that are yet to be done.

We then take the opportunity to tell you a bit about us. We will, for example, outline the basics of our Fiscal House™ approach to retirement income and wealth building, a financial blueprint that includes:

- The Foundation of money that you can lose only if you choose. These financial vehicles provide principal protection, fixed rates, potential interest earnings opportunities based on indexed products participation, and guaranteed lifetime income.
- The Walls are investments with the potential to produce both income and growth with reduced exposure and lower correlation to market volatility.
- The Roof uses investments designed for the continued long-term growth and tactical management of your retirement assets at a risk level with which you are comfortable.

We might also talk in broad strokes about strategies we might explore in future meetings should you honor us in continuing this relationship.

Subsequent meetings will get down to the heavy lifting, the detailed planning we will do together to develop the blueprint for your Fiscal House. We'll then begin building the structure designed to help shelter you over the course of your retirement, one that will be move-in ready at the time you are finally ready to make the big move.

Service after the sale

We sometimes hear clients say their displeasure with an advisor or investment broker comes from a "pitch it and ditch it" approach. Maybe they purchased an insurance policy or made an investment, but then didn't hear anything further from the selling agent. No follow-up, no interest in seeing how things are going. And then one day they get a call out of the blue asking, "Might I talk to you about buying something else?"

At Russell, we believe in staying in continual contact with our clients. Service after the sale is more than just a slogan.

Our team is built around the idea of customer service. Should you ever have a question, a concern, or a change in your life, we take pride in being available to help you on short notice.

And that's just the reactive side to what we do. Our proactive side involves actively monitoring client accounts so that if market conditions dictate that their investments need attention, we can reach out and advise them of our concerns. They don't have to wait until their annual review to address these issues.

An annual progress review is our bare minimum standard for all clients. Some people ask for more than a yearly review, and we are happy to oblige. Other people might say, "Call me only when the world is ending." We understand … but we'd still like to at least see you more often that.

A continuing education program is another big part of what we do. We hold monthly community education events, often dinners for prospective new clients that our current clients can also attend. We do a weekly radio show, "Total Wealth and Wellness Radio," currently on Saturday mornings on Dayton's WHIO 1290 AM and 95.7 FM. We've now branched out into podcasts as well and continue to do quarterly newsletters with our thoughts on current market and economic trends. And, when conditions dictate, you're likely to see unscheduled email advisories from us.

We also believe that all work and no play makes – well, you know the rest. Social activities are another big part of our efforts to stay in touch with people who become more like friends than clients. Our annual client appreciation event is scheduled each October. In October 2023, we celebrated our 20th anniversary with our clients by hosting our client appreciation even at the National Museum of the United States Air Force.

We believe we have a lot to offer at Russell Total Wealth and Wellness.

We hope we've conveyed many of our core beliefs and planning strategies through the course of this book. We hope we've been helpful in showing you things you can do on your own – research you can do over the course of a weekend – that will hopefully give you a better understanding of where you currently stand on the road to retirement. We also hope we've raised some retirement-related issues with which you might need professional help, the kind of guidance we stand ready to provide as you approach the point where you finally decide that five o'clock is finally here.

Russell Total Wealth and Wellness
One Russell Place
Dayton, Ohio 45409
937-320-4733
800-392-4378 (toll free)
E-mail: RTWW@TotalWealthAdvice.com

Acknowledgments

This book, authored by two Sr. Wealth Advisors who are part of a team at Russell Total Wealth and Wellness, would not have happened without the efforts of Ron Russell, the founder of our firm. Previously, a Certified Public Accountant, Ron in 1972 started his own Dayton, Ohio, tax firm that has since expanded to become a retirement planning company whose mission is to help people make great decisions in order to enjoy their best possible retirement.

Ron remains an integral part of all that we do today. He was pushing eighty as this book was being finished, but was still working four days a week. In our time with the firm, we've been able to have one of the greatest mentors any financial advisor could ask for. They say experience is the best teacher, and with Ron we count ourselves fortunate to come to work each day and continue to learn from him.

His son Rob is the visionary in our firm. He's always looking to the future, thinking about what we're capable of doing or how we might do things better. He's always looking at where we might be as opposed to where we are. His ability to look into our company's future is a great balance for the rest of us who concentrate on helping our clients look ahead into what might be in store for them.

Our company wouldn't be where it is today without Ron and Rob Russell. This book most likely would not have been written, its authors not brought together, without them.

We also want to thank all the members of our team at Russell Total Wealth and Wellness. We work with a lot of great team members who give freely of their time in order to help others. Most everyone here is from the town we work in, and it's special to create something in the community that raised us. Our backgrounds in our Dayton home area provide the foundation of what makes us a local/regional wealth management firm as opposed to part of a big, national, institutional broker. We like being a bigger fish in a smaller pond, and we like being able to be of service to the people of our community – the folks we go to church with, the people who used to be our teachers and coaches, the parents of the kids our kids play with. We continue to interact with people who've played such big roles in our past, and that's important to so many people in our firm. People here take it as a badge of honor that we're a grass roots, home-grown firm.

From Curvin Miller IV

A special thank you to my wife Emily, who's been such a big part of my professional life throughout my career. I started at Russell in November of 2004, then met Emily in February of 2005. She's been with me in all the time I've been doing this, including some lean and eager years at the beginning when we would sit around the table trying to figure out what we would do next. She's spent a lot of time listening to me talk about the bad times and good times alike, the constant support person in my life.

To my mom and dad, Curvin III and Louie, who gave me a lot of wisdom in areas beyond the financial services industry. They are not finance people, but what I got from them was a lot of love, as well as the importance of loving other people. They are very special people who are always there for others. I had friends in high school who grew up with only one parent, or maybe didn't have the upbringing I had, but my folks were always there to put an arm around them and remind them that there is a better tomorrow. They were always there to provide motivation and guidance and life lessons for my friends who didn't have the family support we did.

To my kiddos, Curvin V and Colin, who always keep my life interesting. They are brothers who couldn't be more different, but they somehow manage to complement each other perfectly. Right now they are pre-teens who are about to become great young men, and as their father, I couldn't be more proud. We're about to enter some very challenging years, and I look forward to it.

And once again, another special shout out to my special mentor, Ron Russell, who also happens to be my uncle. We're not related by blood – his second marriage was to my aunt – but it seems like I've always been around him from an early age. It seems like I was always interested in anything Ron had going on. When I was in third grade, I brought him to class on show-and-tell day because he could do magic tricks. I learned about life and loving people from my own dad and mom, but I got my financial chops from Ron as a sort of second father-figure.

From Andie Doller

To my daughters, Maddie and Karter: You're my greatest joy and my reason for striving to be my best every day. You inspire me in ways I never would have dreamed possible and I'm so proud of you. YOU are my favorites!

To Mom: You are one of the strongest women I know. Thank you for always being so supportive of my dreams and goals. You are always right there to help me and I'll never be able to say "thank you" nearly enough.

To Nate: I admire you so much. Not just as an amazing brother, entrepreneur, or all around brainiac, but as one of my best friends.

To Meow, Lucy, Sarah and Skom: You are my chosen sisters and I feel so blessed to call you my friends. Thank you for the silly and the serious. They say true friends keep you grounded while lifting you up, and you've proven that to be true time and time again. Cheers to you!

To Gracie: You are brilliant, creative, and curious – a most wonderful combination! Your Prippy loves you.

CURVIN MILLER IV AND ANDIE DOLLER
About the Authors

Curvin Miller IV, a Sr. Vice President and Sr. Wealth Advisor at Russell Total Wealth and Wellness in Dayton, Ohio, has been helping clients navigate the often-confusing world of retirement planning since 2004.

Born and raised in the Dayton area, Curv has a Bachelor of Science in business from Miami (Ohio) University. He also serves as co-host (with Andie Doller) of Total Wealth and Wellness Radio, which can be heard at 8 a.m. Saturdays on 95.7 FM and AM 1290 News Talk Radio, WHIO in Dayton.

A die-hard Columbus Bluejackets fan, Curv plays in a men's hockey league. He also serves as an assistant coach for his son's youth hockey team. Outside of spending time with his family, Curv enjoys golfing, cooking, travel and exercise. Another favorite activity is mountain biking. He is also a former competitive swimmer whose primary events included the breaststroke and individual medley. At the age of 15, he got to train with the Singapore National Team in Singapore.

Curv and his wife, Emily, have two sons, Curvin "V" and Colin, as well as three Yorkies named Chloe, Dublin and Jamison. Curv and his family attend Southbrook Christian Church in Miamisburg, Ohio.

Andie Doller, a Sr. Wealth Advisor at Russell Total Wealth and Wellness, began her career in corporate banking in 1999, and ascended into the financial services sector in 2004.

Andrea Doller has dedicated her professional life to navigating the complexities of financial planning. Andie's passion for the financial field spills out into one of the roles she enjoys most, mentoring and training new Advisors.

"Andie" earned her Associates Degree in Business, then continued her education, going on to receive a BA in Marketing as well. Andie joins Curv Miller Saturdays at 8 a.m. on WHIO as co-host of Total Wealth and Wellness Radio and co-authored best-selling How to Retire in a Weekend, released in 2023 (available on Amazon).

Andie resides in Carlisle with her twin teenage daughters, Maddie and Karter. If you ask Andie though, her favorite child is the family dog, Gunner! Andie is a Jeep lover and, along with her girls, can be found on the weekends making memories doing all things outdoors: hiking, boating, camping, and swimming, just to name a few! It's not all leisure with Andie though, she noted: "I think it's important to instill a service mindset in my girls. We also spend time together volunteering. SICSA and Sleep In Heavenly Peace are our favorites."

www.ingramcontent.com/pod-product-compliance
Lightning Source LLC
Chambersburg PA
CBHW050008230526
45465CB00003BB/1317